GETTING BY IN
GERMAN

Second Edition

EINBAHNSTRASSE

A QUICK BEGINNER'S COURSE FOR
TOURISTS AND BUSINESS PEOPLE

Joachim Kothe

BARRON'S

In cooperation with BBC Languages

First edition for the United States
published 1996 by Barron's Educational Series, Inc.
in cooperation with BBC Languages,
a division of BBC Worldwide, Ltd.,
Woodlands, 80 Wood Lane, London W12 0TT

© Copyright 1992 by Joachim Kothe

Portions of the Reference section of this book from *German at a Glance* by Henry
Strutz.

Library of Congress Catalog Card No. 96-1459
International Standard Book No. 0-8120-9679-7 (book)
0-8120-8441-1 (book and cassettes package)

Library of Congress Cataloging-in-Publication Data

Kothe, Joachim.
  Getting by in German : a quick beginner's course for tourists and business people /
Joachim Kothe.—2nd ed.
    p.   cm.
  Rev. ed. of: Getting by in German / Edith Baer. © 1982.
  ISBN 0-8120-9679-7
  1. German language—Conversation and phrase books—English.
2. German language—Grammar.   I. Baer, Edith. Getting by in German.   II. Title.
PF3121.K64   1996
438.3'421—dc20   96-1459
                                                                    CIP

Printed in Hong Kong
987654321

CONTENTS

INTRODUCTION

Barron's new *Getting by in German* is a quick beginner's course for anyone planning to visit Germany or any other German-speaking country on business or for pleasure. It consists of two audio-cassettes and this book.

Getting by in German will not equip you to hold lengthy conversations in German, but it **will** help you to:

- Make yourself understood in everyday situations, such as ordering a drink, finding your way around, shopping, making a phone call, and so on
- Understand what people may say to you
- Get used to the sounds and patterns of German, a good foundation should you wish to take your German further
- Make new friends and get more out of your trip by 'having a go' at the language.

Getting by in German is based on real-life conversations specially recorded in Hamburg in northern Germany, so you will get used to hearing authentic German right from the start.

THE AUDIOCASSETTES

The cassettes:

- Contain the conversations reproduced in this book
- Explain the language you need to speak and understand in each situation
- Give you plenty of opportunities to repeat words and expressions aloud, answer simple questions and take part in conversations like those you might have abroad
- Allow you to study at your own pace.

THE BOOK

This book includes:

- Key words and phrases used in each unit
- Transcripts of the recorded conversations
- Further word lists for each unit

- Brief explanations of language points
- Exercises to help you practice your skills
- Basic information and tips about life in Germany
- Final test to see if you can *Get by*
- Reference section containing a simple guide to German pronunciation (you can hear this at the end of the second cassette) and useful language notes
- Complete list of words used in the course.

TO MAKE THE MOST OF THE COURSE

- First of all look through the unit in the book to give yourself an idea of what to expect. Then listen to the cassette. There are pauses for you to practice pronunciation, answer questions and take part in conversations. Join in aloud and, if you don't get it quite right the first time, wind back the cassette and listen again. If the pause isn't long enough, you can always use the pause button on your cassette player to extend it. Go through the exercises several times until you can do them with no mistakes.
- When you've worked through the cassette, go back to the book and read the conversation transcripts again, review the explanations and try the exercises.
- Lastly, play the cassettes as often as possible – in the car, working around the house, or on your personal cassette player when shopping or walking the dog.
- One final suggestion: if you're learning with someone else, take advantage of the opportunity to 'act out' the dialogues, repeating them again and again until you can do them without the book. As you get more confident, you can try making variations of your own.

We hope you enjoy *Getting by in German*. And wherever you go in the future in the German-speaking world . . . *Gute Reise und viel Spaß!*

1 MEETING PEOPLE

KEY WORDS AND PHRASES

HELLOS AND GOODBYES

guten Morgen	good morning
guten Tag	good morning, good afternoon (*lit.* good day)
guten Abend	good evening
hallo	hello
(auf) Wiedersehen	(good)bye
tschüs	bye-bye
wie geht's? **wie geht es Ihnen?**	how are you?
danke, gut	fine, thanks

BREAKING THE ICE

wie heißen Sie?	what's your name?
woher kommen Sie?	where are you from?
ich komme/bin aus . . .	I'm from . . .
das ist . . .	this is . . .

ORDERING DRINKS

Herr Ober!	waiter!
ein Kännchen Tee	a pot of tea
eine Cola	a coke
noch zwei Bier	two more beers

bitte	please
danke	thank you

CONVERSATIONS

The following conversations are included on the cassette.
Listen to them carefully. The important words and phrases
are listed above, but look up any other words you don't
understand in the word list following the conversations. The
Explanations section will help you with language points to be
found in the conversations.

OUT AND ABOUT IN HAMBURG

Hello. How are you?

FR. HARRINGTON Guten Tag, Herr Hinze.

HERR HINZE Oh, hallo, Frau Harrington. Wie geht es Ihnen?

FR. HARRINGTON Ach ja, ganz gut. Und Ihnen?

HERR HINZE Danke, gut.

Good morning. Fine, thanks. And you?

FRAU PAGITZ Guten Morgen, Frau Peters.

FRAU PETERS 'n Morgen, Frau Pagitz.

FRAU PAGITZ Wie geht's?

FRAU PETERS Danke, gut. Und Ihnen?

FRAU PAGITZ Och, danke. Es geht.

VISITING FRAU PETERS

Good evening. This is Frau Pagitz.

FRAU PETERS *(answering the doorbell)* Ach, Herr Dr. Göttsch. Guten Abend.

DR. GÖTTSCH	Guten Abend, Frau Peters. Darf ich vorstellen, das ist Frau Pagitz.
FRAU PAGITZ	Guten Abend, Frau Peters.
FRAU PETERS	Guten Abend, Frau Pagitz. Kommen Sie doch bitte rein.

introduce

herein?

Goodbye!

HAMBURGER	Auf Wiedersehen! Wiedersehen! Wiederschauen! Tschüs!

Are you from Hamburg? No, I'm from Speyer.

FRAU PAGITZ	Frau Peters, sind Sie aus Hamburg?
FRAU PETERS	Nein, ich bin nicht aus Hamburg. Ich komme aus Speyer. Das liegt in Rheinland-Pfalz.

What's your name? Where are you from?

FRAU PAGITZ	Wie heißen Sie, bitte?
FRAU BEHRENS	Barbara Behrens.
FRAU PAGITZ	Sind Sie aus Hamburg, Frau Behrens?
FRAU BEHRENS	Nein, ich bin Engländerin.
FRAU PAGITZ	Ach, Sie sind Engländerin!
FRAU BEHRENS	Ja.
FRAU PAGITZ	Woher kommen Sie?
FRAU BEHRENS	Ich komme aus Bristol.

I'm a Hamburger.

FRAU PAGITZ	Sind Sie aus Hamburg?
DR. GÖTTSCH	Ja, ich bin Hamburger.

REFRESHMENTS

In the Alsterpavillon. Waiter! A pot of tea, please. With lemon.

FRAU EVRAHR	Herr Ober!

OBER	Ja, bitte schön?
FRAU EVRAHR	Bitte, ein Kännchen Tee.
OBER	Möchten Sie den Tee mit Sahne oder Zitrone?
FRAU EVRAHR	Gern mit Zitrone. _cream_
OBER	Gerne.

In the bar Die Glocke *(The Bell).*
A coke, a mineral water and a wine. A white one.

FR. HARRINGTON	Herr Ober!
OBER	Ja, bitte?
FR. HARRINGTON	Eine Cola, ein Mineralwasser und ein' Wein, bitte.
OBER	Möchten Sie einen roten oden einen weißen Wein?
FR. HARRINGTON	Einen weißen, bitte.
OBER	Wird gemacht!

Two beers, please. Large ones.

GAST	Herr Ober! Zwei Bier, bitte.
OBER	Große oder kleine?
GAST	Zwei große, bitte.

Two more beers. And two more schnaps as well.

GAST	Herr Ober!
OBER	Ja, bitte?
GAST	Bringen Sie noch zwei Bier, bitte.
OBER	Ja, gerne.
GAST	Und noch zwei Kurze dazu.
OBER	Ist in Ordnung.

Six-year-old Berthe counts up to ten.

BERTHE	Eins, zwei, drei, vier, fünf, sechs, sieben, acht, neun, zehn.
FR. HARRINGTON	Noch einmal, ein kleines bißchen langsamer, bitte . . .

BERTHE	Eins, zwei, drei, vier, fünf, sechs, sieben, acht, neun, zehn.
FR. HARRINGTON	Schön hast du das gemacht, Berthe.

WORD LIST

ganz gut	pretty good
und Ihnen?	and you?
es geht	not too bad
darf ich vorstellen . . . ?	may I introduce . . . ?
kommen Sie rein	come in
das liegt in . . .	that's (located) in . . .
bitte schön?	yes, please?
möchten Sie . . . ?	would you like . . . ?
mit Sahne oder Zitrone?	with cream or lemon?
einen roten oder einen weißen?	a red one or a white one?
wird gemacht	right away
der Gast	guest
große oder kleine?	large or small?
bringen Sie mir . . .	bring me . . .
zwei Kurze	two 'shots'
dazu	as well
noch einmal	once again
ein bißchen langsamer	a bit more slowly
schön hast du das gemacht	you did that (very) nicely

EXPLANATIONS

HELLO

Between getting up and about midday: *guten Morgen!*
All day until 5 or 6 p.m.: *guten Tag!*
In the evening: *guten Abend!*
Informally to people you know: *hallo!*

In practice the *guten* is often swallowed, so you'll hear: *'n Morgen! 'n Tag! 'n Abend!*

Depending on which part of Germany you're in, you may come across regional variations like the north German *Moin! ('n Morgen!)* and *Tach! ('n Tag)*. Especially in southern Germany and Austria, people say: *grüß Gott! (lit.* 'greet God!').

GOODBYE

Auf Wiedersehen! (or *Wiedersehen!*) and *auf Wiederschauen!* (or *Wiederschauen!*) mean literally 'until we see each other again'. More casually you can say *tschüs!,* which is like 'bye-bye!'.

HOW ARE YOU?

To find out ask: *wie geht es Ihnen?* or *wie geht's?*
Mostly you can answer: *danke, gut* (fine, thanks) or: *danke, es geht* (not too bad, thanks).
If you really are under the weather, say: *danke, nicht gut* (not very well). In which case you might get the reply: *gute Besserung!* (get well soon!)

INTRODUCTIONS

To introduce someone else, start with:
das ist . . . this is . . .
You'd say:
das ist | *Herr/Frau/Fräulein . . .*
| Mr/Mrs/Miss . . .
| *Herr Doktor/Frau Doktor . . .*
Like Dr. Göttsch, you can put *darf ich vorstellen?* (may I introduce?) in front:
Darf ich vorstellen? Das ist Frau Pagitz.

To introduce yourself:
ich bin . . . I'm . . .
or: *ich heiße . . .* my name's . . .
If you haven't been introduced, you could ask:
wie heißen Sie, bitte? what's your name, please?

WHERE ARE YOU FROM?

To find out, ask:
sind Sie aus . . . ? are you from . . . ?
woher kommen Sie? where do you come from?
To answer, you can say:
ja/nein yes/no
ich komme/bin (nicht) aus . . . I'm (not) from . . .

NATIONALITIES

Are you Scottish? Welsh? American? Irish? English? Then, if you're a man, say:
ich bin . . . Schotte, Waliser, Amerikaner, Ire, Engländer
If you're a woman, the nationality usually ends with *-in:*
ich bin . . . Schottin, Waliserin, Amerikanerin, Irin, Engländerin

ORDERING DRINKS

Just say what you want, and add 'please':

ein Kännchen Tee,	
ein Wein,	*bitte*
noch zwei Bier,	
eine Cola,	

You may be offered a choice:
mit Sahne oder Zitrone?
einen roten oder einen weißen?
große oder kleine?
Then simply repeat the option you'd like:
große, bitte

HAMBURGER OR *HAMBURGER*?

It's not usually difficult to tell whether people are talking about fast food or an inhabitant of Hamburg!

What do you suppose a resident of Frankfurt is called? And what did President Kennedy say in Berlin?

'THE' AND 'A'

German has three kinds of nouns: masculine (m.), feminine (f.) and neuter (n.). The words you use for 'the' and 'a' vary accordingly:

	MASCULINE	FEMININE	NEUTER
the	**der** *Tag*	**die** *Dame*	**das** *Bier*
a	**ein** *Tag*	**eine** *Dame*	**ein** *Bier*

Unfortunately there's not much logic about which words are which gender. It's best to learn them as you go along. Don't worry if you get it wrong. You'll still be understood.

'YOU' AND 'I'

In this chapter you've met several verbs. With *ich* (I) the ending is usually -*e* and with *Sie* (you) it's usually -*en*:

	gehen	*kommen*	*heißen*	*bringen*
	to go	to come	to be called	to bring
ich:	*gehe*	*komme*	*heiße*	*bringe*
Sie:	*gehen*	*kommen*	*heißen*	*bringen*

But there's an important exception:
sein (to be): *ich bin   Sie sind*

CAPITAL LETTERS

One peculiarity of German is that you write nouns with a capital letter: *das Bier, der Abend*. *Sie* and *Ihnen* also have a capital when they mean 'you':
sind Sie aus Hamburg?
wie geht es Ihnen?

THE *UMLAUT* AND *ß*

German has four letters that don't exist in any other language: *ä; ö; ü;* and *ß*. The two dots over the vowels, called an *Umlaut*, change the vowels' sound. The ß stands for 'ss'.
grüß Gott!   *bitte schön*
ein Kännchen Tee   große oder kleine?

NUMBERS 1–10

eins, zwei, drei, vier, fünf, sechs, sieben, acht, neun, zehn

If you don't understand them (or anything else!) the first time, get them repeated: *noch einmal, bitte*   more slowly: *langsamer!*

EXERCISES

HELLO AND GOODBYE

1a You come into your hotel at 2 p.m. How do you greet the porter?
  b You return at 7 p.m. What do you say?
  c You meet your friend Dieter. Say hello.
  d And how do you say goodbye to him?

HOW ARE YOU?

2 You meet Herr Meier in the street. How does your conversation go?

SIE	_____ .
HERR MEIER	Ach, hallo! Wie geht's?
SIE	_____
	und _____ ?
HERR MEIER	_____ , auch _____ . (*auch* = also)

WHERE ARE YOU FROM?

3 You get into conversation with a passenger on the train. What do you say?

PASSAGIER	Sind Sie aus Holland?
SIE	(No, you're a Scot.)
PASSAGIER	Sind Sie aus Edinburgh?
SIE	(From Edinburgh? No, you're *not* from Edinburgh!)
PASSAGIER	Woher kommen Sie denn?
SIE	(You're from Glasgow.)

ORDERING DRINKS

4 In a bar you order a small beer for yourself and then a whiskey on the rocks for your friend:

SIE	_____ !
OBER	Ja, bitte schön?
SIE	_____ .
OBER	Ein großes oder ein kleines?
SIE	_____ . Und _____ .
OBER	Möchten Sie den Whisky mit Eis oder mit Wasser?
SIE	_____ .
OBER	Gerne.

MORE DRINKS

5 You've invited a German friend and his daughter to the Café Reckers. What do you say?

SIE	(Would you like coffee?)
FREUND	Nein. Ich nehme Tee.
SIE	(With lemon or milk?)
FREUND	Mit Milch, bitte. Und Sie? Möchten Sie auch Tee?
SIE	(No, I'd like coffee.)
TOCHTER	Und ich möchte . . .
SIE	(Would you like tea?)
TOCHTER	Nein, Tee nicht.
SIE	(Would you like hot chocolate?)
TOCHTER	Oh ja, bitte.
SIE	(A small or large cup?)
TOCHTER	Eine große Tasse, bitte.
SIE	(Call the waiter.)
OBER	Ja, bitte?
SIE	(Order a pot of tea, a pot of coffee and a large cup of hot chocolate.)
OBER	Ja, gerne.

Café Reckers

HEISSE GETRÄNKE

Kaffee (Kännchen) 5,85 DM

Tee (Kännchen) mit Zitrone oder Milch 5,85 DM

Heiße Schokolade

(kleine Tasse) 2,75 DM

(große Tasse) 5,– DM

Irish Coffee 7,65 DM

WORTH KNOWING

SAYING HELLO

When you go into somewhere like a shop, restaurant or office, you generally say *guten Morgen/Tag/Abend!* and, when you leave, *auf Wiedersehen!* On a more personal level people usually shake hands when they say hello or goodbye. Sometimes, even at large gatherings, you go around and shake hands with everybody, introducing yourself where necessary. The same may happen at business meetings. With good friends you might exchange kisses.

FIRST NAME OR SURNAME?

In Germany it's not as common as in English-speaking countries to be on first-name terms right away, though this varies with the situation and the age group of the people. The best advice is to listen carefully to what the others do, then do the same. If in doubt, choose *Herr, Frau* or *Fräulein*. But be careful! Many unmarried women regard being called *Fräulein* as a form of discrimination, so if in doubt say *Frau*.

GETTING A DRINK

In Germany you'll find a large variety of snack bars (*der Imbiß*), bars (*die Kneipe, die Gaststätte*), cafés (*das Café, die Konditorei*), and restaurants (*das Restaurant*). There are virtually no restrictions on opening hours and licensing laws are very liberal.

You go to an *Imbiß* for a quick stand-up snack or drink, usually tea, coffee, a soft drink or beer. In bars you get every sort of drink, although usually only one or two kinds of beer are on draft. Especially in northern Germany, you often drink a 'shot' (*ein Kurzer, ein Klarer*) along with your beer.

Mostly this is a clear (*klar*) ice-cold *Schnaps* made from grain.
It's supposed to warm up the stomach for the cold beer to
come. On the other hand some would say that's just an
excuse! Bars don't always serve food, and if they do, there'll
be a rather limited menu.

In cafés you'll find mainly coffee, tea, pastries, and cakes but
alcoholic and soft drinks are also served, and some offer light
snack-type meals as well. Warning: coffee and tea may be more
expensive than in the United States. Service charge (*Bedienung*)
and value-added tax or VAT (*Mehrwertsteuer*) are usually included
in the price on the menu, but the waiter still expects a tip of up
to 10 percent on top of the bill!

THE ALSTERPAVILLON

The Alster is a tributary of the river Elbe dammed up to form
two huge lakes, one of them the *Binnenalster,* in downtown
Hamburg. The *Alsterpavillon,* built in 1799 by a French émigré,
is a café and restaurant beautifully situated on the *Binnenalster*
and a favorite rendezvous for locals and tourists alike.

DRINKS

Most alcoholic drinks are the same in German as in English
(*whiskey, gin, sherry*, etc.), but here are some others you might
like to try:

Limonade	carbonated soft drink
Sprudel	carbonated soft drink (n. Ger.); mineral water (s. Ger.)
Alsterwasser (n. Ger.)	shandy ⎫
Radler (s. Ger.)	shandy ⎬ beer and ginger ale
Moorwasser	citrus-flavored carbonated soft drink with cola
Apfelsaft	apple juice
Orangensaft	orange juice

Traubensaft	grape juice
(heiße) Schokolade	(hot) chocolate
Malzbier	dark, sweet malt beer with very little alcohol
Bier alkoholfrei	low–alcohol beer★

★Low-alcohol beer may be declared alcohol-free (*alkoholfrei*) in Germany but it still contains a small percentage of alcohol. In addition you can get 'light' beers which usually have about half the alcohol content of ordinary German beer.

2 SHOPPING

KEY WORDS AND PHRASES

SAYING WHAT YOU WANT

ich hätte gern . . .	I'd like . . .
ich möchte . . .	
haben Sie . . . ?	have you . . . ?
das ist alles	that's all
200 Gramm (Käse)	200 grams (of cheese)
ein Pfund (Tomaten)	a pound (of tomatoes)
ein Kilo (Bananen)	a kilo (of bananas)
ein Paket (Schwarzbrot)	a package (of rye bread)

THE SALESCLERK MAY ASK:

was darf ich Ihnen geben?	what would you like?
was kann ich für Sie tun?	may I help you?
was hätten Sie gern?	
was hätten Sie noch gerne?	
haben Sie sonst noch einen Wunsch?	would you like anything else?

PAYING

was macht das?	how much does that come to?

CONVERSATIONS

FOOD SHOPPING
. . . .

200 grams of Dutch cheese, please. In one piece.

VERKÄUFERIN	Guten Tag.
FRAU EVRAHR	Guten Tag.
VERKÄUFERIN	Was darf ich Ihnen geben?
FRAU EVRAHR	Bitte zweihundert Gramm Holländer.
VERKÄUFERIN	Möchten Sie es im Stück oder geschnitten?
FRAU EVRAHR	Im Stück.
VERKÄUFERIN	Im Stück . . .
FRAU EVRAHR	Ja.
VERKÄUFERIN	Ja.

A pound of tomatoes, please. Nice ripe ones.

VERKÄUFERIN	Guten Abend. Was kann ich für Sie tun?
FRAU EVRAHR	Ein Pfund Tomaten, bitte.
VERKÄUFERIN	Gerne.
FRAU EVRAHR	Schön reife, bitte.
VERKÄUFERIN	*(weighs them)* Haben Sie sonst noch einen Wunsch?
FRAU EVRAHR	Ja, ein Kilo Bananen.
VERKÄUFERIN	Gerne.

Six rolls and a package of rye bread.

FRAU ANTHES	Guten Tag. Was hätten Sie denn gerne?
FRAU EVRAHR	Sechs Brötchen, bitte.
FRAU ANTHES	Sechs Brötchen, ja . . . *(puts them in a bag)* Und was hätten Sie denn noch gerne?
FRAU EVRAHR	Schwarzbrot. Ein Paket Schwarzbrot.
FRAU ANTHES	Ein Paket Schwarzbrot . . . *(takes down the package)* Sonst noch einen Wunsch?
FRAU EVRAHR	Das ist alles.
FRAU ANTHES	Danke schön.

WINE AND ROSES

I'd like some roses. Seven yellow ones, please.

FRAU EVRAHR   Ich hätte gerne Rosen.

FRAU WITTROCK   Und welche Farbe darf es sein?

FRAU EVRAHR   Gelbe.

FRAU WITTROCK   Ja. Und wieviel?

FRAU EVRAHR   Sieben Stück.

FRAU WITTROCK   Gern.

A bottle of wine, please. Have you got a Moselle?

FR. HARRINGTON   Ich möchte gerne eine Flasche Wein.

HERR PLUSCHKE   Bitte schön, meine Dame. Möchten Sie einen Weißwein oder einen Rotwein?

FR. HARRINGTON   Einen Weißwein.

HERR PLUSCHKE   Weißwein.

FR. HARRINGTON   Haben Sie einen Mosel?

HERR PLUSCHKE   Hab' ich, natürlich. Ich habe hier zum Beispiel einen Marienburger Riesling für acht Mark fünfundneunzig.

FR. HARRINGTON   Das klingt gut. Den nehme ich.

HERR PLUSCHKE   Ja. Bitte schön.

POSTCARDS AND STAMPS

These two postcards, please. Have you got stamps?

FRAU EVRAHR   Guten Tag. Diese zwei Karten, bitte.

FRAU THEEL   Ja, danke schön. Das macht zwei Mark.

FRAU EVRAHR   Haben Sie Briefmarken?

FRAU THEEL   Tut mir leid. Hab' ich leider nicht.

How much is a postcard to Great Britain?

FRAU EVRAHR   Wieviel kostet eine Postkarte nach Großbritannien?

FRAU WEHLING   Sechzig Pfennig.

FRAU EVRAHR   Dann nehme ich sechs Briefmarken zu
              sechzig, bitte.
FRAU WEHLING Sechs Briefmarken zu sechzig, gerne . . .
              (handing her the stamps) Bitte schön. Das
              macht drei Mark und sechzig, bitte.

PAYING

**Frau Evrahr is paying for the roses. How much does that
come to?**

FRAU EVRAHR   Was macht das?
FRAU WITTROCK Neun Mark und zehn.
FRAU EVRAHR   *(paying)* Zehn Mark.
FRAU WITTROCK Danke schön. Und neunzig Pfennig zurück.
FRAU EVRAHR   Ja. Danke.

Paying for the rolls and rye bread.

FRAU EVRAHR   Und was macht das?
FRAU ANTHES   Das macht jetzt fünf Mark und
              fünfundneunzig.
FRAU EVRAHR   Gut.
FRAU ANTHES   Fünf Mark fünfundneunzig, und fünf *(giving
              the change)*.
FRAU EVRAHR   Danke sehr.

CASHING TRAVELER'S CHECKS

I'd like to cash some traveler's checks.

HR. HASENJÄGER Ich möchte gern Reiseschecks einlösen.
FRAU WITTKE   Ja, gerne. Wenn Sie dann hier bitte einmal
                unterschreiben würden.
HR. HASENJÄGER Hier?
FRAU WITTKE   Ja.

WORD LIST

die Verkäuferin	salesclerk
im Stück oder geschnitten?	in one piece or sliced?
welche Farbe darf es sein?	which color would you like?
wieviel?/wie viele?	how much?/how many?
meine Dame	madam
hab' ich	yes, I have
natürlich	of course
ich habe hier . . .	I have here . . .
zum Beispiel	for example
das klingt gut	that sounds good
den nehme ich	I'll take it
das macht	that's (that comes to)
tut mir leid	sorry
leider nicht	I'm afraid not
wieviel kostet . . . ?	how much does . . . cost?
dann nehme ich . . .	then I'll take . . .
zurück	change (*lit.* back)
jetzt	now
wenn Sie dann hier bitte einmal unterschreiben würden	if you'd just sign here then

EXPLANATIONS

SHOP TALK

Salesclerks have their own favorite ways of asking what you'd like:

was darf ich Ihnen geben?
was kann ich für Sie tun?
was hätten Sie denn gerne?
was darf es sein?
kann ich Ihnen helfen?

And, when they've helped you with the first item, they'll probably ask, 'anything else?':

haben Sie sonst noch einen Wunsch?
sonst noch etwas?
darf es noch etwas sein?
was hätten Sie noch gerne?

You see that each of those questions contains the word *noch*. If you hear *noch*, you'll know they're asking if you want more.

To ask for what you want, name the item and add 'please':

sechs Brötchen, bitte
bitte, zweihundert Gramm Holländer

or you can start with 'I'd like':

ich hätte gerne Rosen
ich möchte gerne eine Flasche Wein

And to check if they've got something:

haben Sie Briefmarken?
haben Sie einen Mosel?

QUANTITIES

By law, prices for unpackaged foods have to be given either per kilogram (1000g) or per 100g. Even on packaged foods you'll always find the price for one kilogram to allow comparison. Very often you buy food by the pound, which in Germany means 500g or half a kilo:

a pound:	*ein Pfund Tomaten*
a quarter pound:	*ein Viertelpfund (125g) Holländer*

Or you might want:

a package:	*ein Paket Schwarzbrot*
a can:	*eine Dose (Büchse) Sardinen*
a carton:	*eine Tüte Milch*

Remember that in German you don't need a word for 'of':

ein Kilo Äpfel	a kilo of apples
eine Flasche Wein	a bottle of wine

COLORS

blau	blue	*grün*	green
braun	brown	*rot*	red
gelb	yellow	*schwarz*	black
grau	gray	*weiß*	white

SECHS STÜCK, BITTE

Stück means 'piece', but you can also use it to say how many of something you want:

wie viele Rosen?	*sieben Stück, bitte*
wie viele Brötchen?	*sechs Stück, bitte*
wie viele Postkarten?	*drei Stück, bitte*

MORE ABOUT NUMBERS

To understand prices you need to know numbers. There's a full list on page 96, but here are a few points to help you on the way:

- 11 and 12 are *elf* and *zwölf*
- The teens end with *-zehn* and the tens (except *dreißig*) with *-zig*:

4 *vier*	14 *vierzehn*	40 *vierzig*
5 *fünf*	15 *fünfzehn*	50 *fünfzig*

- From 20 on, Germans say 'one and twenty', 'two and twenty', etc.:

einundzwanzig, zweiundzwanzig, dreiundzwanzig, vierundzwanzig

- If you need to write them out, numbers are written as one word!

MONEY MATTERS

The *Deutsche Mark* (DM) or *die Mark* consists of 100 pfennigs (*der Pfennig*). Prices are spoken as they are in English:
$1.20:   one dollar (and) twenty (cents)
1,20 DM: *eine Mark (und) zwanzig (Pfennige)*
But you'll notice that, when prices are written, there's a decimal point between the dollars and cents but a comma between the marks and pfennigs.

German currency comes in the following denominations:
Coins: 1 *Pfennig*, 2 *Pfennig*, 5 *Pfennig*, 10 *Pfennig*, 50 *Pfennig*, 1 *Mark*, 2 *Mark*, 5 *Mark*
Notes: 5 *Mark*, 10 *Mark*, 20 *Mark*, 50 *Mark*, 100 *Mark*, 200 *Mark*, 500 *Mark*, 1000 *Mark*.

EXERCISES

YOUR SHOPPING LIST

1   *Bitte schön?* On your shopping list are:
    2 postcards
    500g of Edam cheese *(Edamer)*
    8 rolls
    a package of cookies *(Kekse)*
    5 ròses
    a bottle of red wine
    a pound of apples *(Äpfel)*
    a carton of milk
Ask for them as simply as possible.

2   *Was macht das?* How would you write these prices in figures?
zwei Mark siebenunddreißig
vierundzwanzig Mark elf
siebzehn Mark dreiundvierzig

AT THE DELICATESSEN
. . . .

3 You are out shopping. Your first stop is at the delicatessen for 300g of Dutch cheese. What do you say to the clerk?

VERKÄUFERIN   Was kann ich für Sie tun?

SIE   _____ .

VERKÄUFERIN   Im Stück oder geschnitten?

SIE   (You want it sliced.)

VERKÄUFERIN   Bitte sehr.

SIE   _____ .

THE FRUIT STAND
. . . .

Tomaten	kg 3,99 DM
Orangen	Stück 0,75 DM
Bananen	kg 2,70 DM
Äpfel	kg 2,80 DM
Kiwis	Stück 0,60 DM
Birnen	kg 2,95 DM

4 You go to the marketplace. The fruit looks good so you decide to buy some. What do you say?

VERKÄUFER   Was darf ich Ihnen geben?

SIE   (1kg of tomatoes, please.)

VERKÄUFER   Gern. Sonst noch etwas?

SIE   (Yes, 500g of bananas.)

VERKÄUFER   Ja. Und sonst noch etwas?

SIE   (Does he have kiwi fruit?)

VERKÄUFER   Ja, wie viele möchten Sie denn?

SIE   (Eight, please.)

VERKÄUFER   So, bitte schön.

5 *Und was macht das?* Look at the vendor's list to work out how much you have to pay.

AT THE POST OFFICE

6 You want to write home, so on to the post office (postcards you buy from a post office are blank and have a printed stamp). What do you say to the clerk?

BEAMTIN	Kann ich Ihnen helfen?
SIE	(How much is a letter, *der Brief,* to England?)
BEAMTIN	Eine Mark.
SIE	(You'd like three stamps, please.)
BEAMTIN	Bitte schön. Sonst noch etwas?
SIE	(Ask if she's got postcards.)
BEAMTIN	Ja, hab' ich. Wie viele möchten Sie denn?
SIE	(Four. Ask how much a postcard costs.)
BEAMTIN	60 Pfennig.
SIE	(How much does that come to, please?)
BEAMTIN	Drei Mark und zwei Mark vierzig, das sind fünf Mark vierzig.
SIE	(Hand her the money.)
BEAMTIN	Vielen Dank. Und vierundvierzig sechzig zurück. Auf Wiedersehen.
SIE	(Thank you and goodbye.)

7 You pay with a 50 DM note. What's the smallest number of coins and notes you can get as change? (see p.28)

CASHING A TRAVELER'S CHECK

8 You're running short of money. So you go into the bank to cash a traveler's check (*einen Reisescheck*) for 400 DM.

ANGESTELLTER	Guten Tag.
SIE	_____ .
ANGESTELLTER	Ja, gerne. Unterschreiben Sie bitte hier.
SIE	(Here?)
ANGESTELLTER	Ja bitte . . . So, das macht dann dreihundert-sechsundneunzig Mark fünfzig. Bitte sehr.
SIE	_____ .

9 How many marks did he give you?
10 How much commission did he charge?

SHOPPING HOURS

From Monday to Friday stores in Germany are usually open
from 9 a.m. to 6:30 p.m. Some food shops or kiosks may be
open earlier, while small shops might be closed for one or two
hours during lunchtime. On Thursdays most stores downtown
are open until 8:30 p.m. On Saturdays stores close at noon or
2 p.m., but the first Saturday of the month is *langer Samstag*
(lit. 'long Saturday'), which means they stay open in summer
until 4:30 and in winter until 6 p.m.

MAILING YOUR LETTERS AND POSTCARDS

Stamps are available at post offices (or sometimes from small
stationery or souvenir shops). Ordinary letters and postcards
to other EC countries cost the same as mail within Germany.
But postcards cost less than letters.

Mailboxes are yellow and in towns and cities are emptied
several times a day. Telephone booths are also yellow,
although there are plans to change them to white in the near
future.

Post offices are generally closed between 12 noon and
3 p.m.

AT THE BAKERY

There's an enormous variety of bread and rolls in German
bakeries. There are about twenty different kinds of rolls,

ranging from soft rolls, poppy seed rolls (*Mohnbrötchen*) and rye rolls (*Roggenbrötchen*) to rolls with onions (*Zwiebeln*) or sunflower seeds (*Sonnenblumensamen*) inside. Often they're baked from the whole grain (*Vollkornbrötchen*) or from more than one kind of grain (*Mehrkornbrötchen*). There are about the same number of bread varieties, which are all worth a try. Bread varies from white (*Weißbrot*) to very dark (*Schwarzbrot*). It comes in all shapes and sizes, and in many different flavors. Try *Kümmelbrot* (with caraway seeds), *Zwiebelbrot* (with onions) or *Sonnenblumenbrot* (with sunflower seeds), for example.

GERMAN WINE

As with bread, the choice of wines is enormous and you'll never manage to taste them all. Most wines come from the Rhine or Moselle regions. German wines are mostly white; only in a very few areas, such as the Ahr, is red wine grown.

Herr Pluschke offered Frau Harrington a 'Marienburger Riesling' from the Moselle region. Riesling is a traditional grape, called 'The Queen of Grapes', *Königin der Trauben*.

CHANGING MONEY

You can change cash, traveler's checks, or Eurochecks at most banks and post offices. Additionally there are a growing number of automatic teller machines (ATMs) that accept foreign debit and credit cards.

In stores the use of credit cards is not as widespread as in the UK or USA. Smaller shops often don't accept them and even in department stores you may be sent to a different check-out if you want to pay with 'plastic'. You can't buy train tickets with credit cards, but they're useful for renting a car, eating out, or paying your hotel bill.

3 FINDING SOMEWHERE TO STAY

KEY WORDS AND PHRASES

RESERVING A HOTEL ROOM

ich möchte ein Zimmer reservieren	I'd like to reserve a room
ein Doppelzimmer oder ein Einzelzimmer?	a double room or a single room?
mit Dusche oder mit Bad?	with shower or with bath?

FOR HOW LONG?

für . . .	for . . .
eine Nacht	one night
zwei Nächte	two nights
eine Woche	a week
drei Tage	three days

AT THE CAMPGROUND

haben Sie noch (Zelt) Plätze frei?	do you still have any (tent) sites available?
wir haben . . .	we have . . .
ein Zelt	a tent
einen Wohnwagen	a motor home

CONVERSATIONS

AT THE TOURIST INFORMATION CENTER

I'd like to reserve a double room. With shower.

HERR HINZE	Ich möchte ein Zimmer reservieren.
FRAU HERBST	Ja, gern. Möchten Sie ein Doppelzimmer oder ein Einzelzimmer?
HERR HINZE	Ein Doppelzimmer.
FRAU HERBST	Mit Dusche oder mit Bad?
HERR HINZE	Mit Dusche.
FRAU HERBST	Ja, und für wie viele Nächte möchten Sie bleiben?
HERR HINZE	Für zwei Nächte.

A single room. If possible with bath. For a week.

FRAU PAGITZ	Ich möchte gerne ein Zimmer reservieren.
FRAU HERBST	Was für ein Zimmer möchten Sie reservieren, ein Einzelzimmer oder ein Doppelzimmer?
FRAU PAGITZ	Ein Einzelzimmer.
FRAU HERBST	Ein Einzelzimmer mit Dusche oder mit Bad?
FRAU PAGITZ	Wenn es geht, mit Bad.
FRAU HERBST	Und für wie viele Nächte möchten Sie bleiben?
FRAU PAGITZ	Für eine Woche.
FRAU HERBST	Und wie ist, bitte, Ihr Name?
FRAU PAGITZ	Pagitz.
FRAU HERBST	Gut, Frau Pagitz, ich kann Ihnen ein Zimmer anbieten im Hotel am Dammtor.
FRAU PAGITZ	Und was kostet es?
FRAU HERBST	Das Zimmer kostet neunzig Mark.
FRAU PAGITZ	Ja, das geht.

AT THE HOTEL

Have you got a room? A single with bath, please.

FRAU DEBUS	Haben Sie ein Zimmer frei?
EMPFANG	Was hätten Sie denn gerne? Ein Einzelzimmer oder ein Doppelzimmer?
FRAU DEBUS	Ein Einzelzimmer mit Bad, bitte . . .

I've reserved a room. For two nights.

HERR BESSEN	Mein Name ist Bessen. Ich habe ein Zimmer reserviert.
FRAU STORM	Ja. Herzlich willkommen, Herr Bessen.
HERR BESSEN	Danke schön.
FRAU STORM	Das war ein Einzelzimmer für zwei Nächte.
HERR BESSEN	Ja.
FRAU STORM	Wenn ich Sie gerade noch bitten darf, sich hier einzutragen.
HERR BESSEN	Ja.
FRAU STORM	Adresse . . .
HERR BESSEN	Ja.
FRAU STORM	Und Unterschrift.

*This is your key. Room 75 on the first floor.**

FRAU KRÜGER	Dürfte ich Sie bitten, sich einzutragen?
HERR KOTHE	Ja, sicher.
FRAU KRÜGER	Danke.
HERR KOTHE	*(handing back the form)* Bitte sehr.
FRAU KRÜGER	Danke sehr. Das ist Ihr Zimmerschlüssel. Zimmer fünfundsiebzig in der ersten Etage.

This is room 75. I'd like breakfast in my room, please.

FRAU KRÜGER	*(answering the phone)* Empfang, guten Morgen.
HERR KOTHE	Guten Morgen. Hier ist Zimmer fünfundsiebzig. Ich hätte gern ein Frühstück aufs Zimmer.

* The 'first' floor is one flight up; the 'second' floor = our third floor; etc.

FRAU KRÜGER	Mit Kaffee oder Tee?
HERR KOTHE	Kaffee, bitte.
FRAU KRÜGER	Haben Sie sonst noch irgendwelche extra Wünsche?
HERR KOTHE	Nein, danke.
FRAU KRÜGER	Bitte sehr. Das Frühstück kommt dann sofort.
HERR KOTHE	Vielen Dank. Auf Wiederhören.
FRAU KRÜGER	Wiederhören.

Can you call me a taxi, please? Room 75.

HERR KOTHE	Können Sie mir bitte ein Taxi bestellen?
FRAU KRÜGER	Aber sehr gerne. Wie ist, bitte, Ihre Zimmernummer?
HERR KOTHE	Fünfundsiebzig.
FRAU KRÜGER	*(phoning for a taxi)* Guten Morgen, Hotel Bellevue. Ich bräuchte eine Taxe auf Zimmer fünfundsiebzig. Danke. *(to Herr Kothe)* Die Taxe kommt sofort.

May I have my key, please?

HERR BESSEN	Darf ich meinen Schlüssel bitte haben?
FRAU STORM	Ja. Und welche Zimmernummer?
HERR BESSEN	Dreihunderteinundzwanzig.
FRAU STORM	Ja. *(handing him the key)* So, bitte schön, Herr Bessen.
HERR BESSEN	Danke schön.

I'd like the bill, please. I'm paying by credit card.

HERR KOTHE	Ich hätte gern die Rechnung.
FRAU KRÜGER	Wie ist bitte Ihre Zimmernummer?
HERR KOTHE	Fünfundsiebzig.
FRAU KRÜGER	Danke. Kommt etwas aus der Minibar dazu?
HERR KOTHE	Ja. Ich hatte einen Whisky.
FRAU KRÜGER	Danke schön. Und wie möchten Sie bezahlen?

HERR KOTHE   Mit Kreditkarte, bitte.

FRAU KRÜGER   Ja, danke. *(takes the imprint)* Dürfte ich Sie
                 bitten, zu unterschreiben?

AT THE CAMPGROUND

*I'm here with a motor home. Do you still have spaces
available?*

HR. LÜDERMANN Schön' guten Tag, kann ich Ihnen helfen?

HERR HINZE   Ja. Ich bin hier mit einem Wohnwagen.
                 Haben Sie noch Plätze frei?

HR. LÜDERMANN Ja. Wir haben noch Plätze zur Verfügung.

HERR HINZE   Wir möchten gerne drei Tage bleiben, ist das
                 möglich?

HR. LÜDERMANN Das wäre möglich, ja.

HERR HINZE   Und was kostet das?

HR. LÜDERMANN Wie viele Personen sind Sie?

HERR HINZE   Wir sind zwei Erwachsene und zwei Kinder.

HR. LÜDERMANN Pro Erwachsener bezahlen Sie vier Mark, pro
                 Kind drei Mark, für den Wohnwagen zwölf
                 Mark fünfzig und für den PKW vier Mark.

*Do you still have tent sites available? We have two
bikes.*

FRAU PAGITZ   Haben Sie noch Zeltplätze frei?

HR. LÜDERMANN Wir haben noch Zeltplätze zur Verfügung.
                 Wie groß ist denn Ihr Zelt?

FRAU PAGITZ   Es ist ein Zweipersonenzelt.

HR. LÜDERMANN Sind Sie zwei Personen?

FRAU PAGITZ   Ja.

HR. LÜDERMANN Haben Sie ein Fahrzeug dabei?

FRAU PAGITZ   Ja, wir haben zwei Fahrräder.

WORD LIST

bleiben	to stay
was für . . . ?	what kind of . . . ?
Ihr Name	your name
ich kann . . . anbieten	I can offer . . .
das geht	that's OK
was hätten Sie denn gern?	what (kind of room) would you like?
herzlich willkommen!	you're very welcome!
wenn ich Sie gerade noch bitten darf . . .	if I can just ask you . . .
sich hier einzutragen	to register here
die Adresse	address
die Unterschrift	signature
dürfte ich Sie bitten . . . ?	could I ask you . . . ?
sicher	certainly
der Empfang	reception desk
sonst noch irgendwelche extra Wünsche	any other extra requests
sofort	right away
(auf) Wiederhören	goodbye (on the phone)
Ihre Zimmernummer	your room number
ich bräuchte . . .	I need, please . . .
etwas aus der Minibar	anything from the minibar
ich hatte . . .	I had . . .
bezahlen	to pay
unterschreiben	to sign
der Campingplatz	campground
zur Verfügung	available
das wäre möglich	that would be possible
wie viele Personen?	how many people?
zwei Erwachsene	two adults
zwei Kinder	two children
pro . . .	per . . .

der PKW (Personenkraftwagen)	car
der PKW (Personenkraftwagen)	car
das Zelt	tent
das Fahrzeug	vehicle
zwei Fahrräder	two bicycles
der Platzwart	campground manager

EXPLANATIONS

CHECKING IN

Are rooms/spaces available?
haben Sie Zimmer/(Zelt)Plätze frei?
If you've reserved a room in advance:
ich habe ein Zimmer reserviert
If you want a room on the spot or for a future date:
ich möchte ein Zimmer reservieren

What sort of room?
ein Einzelzimmer oder ein Doppelzimmer
mit Bad oder mit Dusche
mit zwei Betten (though rooms with twin beds are not often
available in German hotels!)

At the campground:

wir haben | *ein Zelt*
| *einen Wohnwagen*

wir sind | *zwei Erwachsene*
| *zwei Erwachsene und zwei Kinder*

How long do you want to stay?

für | *eine Nacht, zwei Nächte*
| *eine Woche, zwei Wochen*

And how much is it?
was kostet es? or *wieviel kostet es?*

WIEVIEL? WIE VIELE?

wieviel? (how much?) is written as one word, *wie viele?* (how many?) as two:

wieviel kostet es?

wie viele Personen sind Sie?

But in spoken German people often say *wieviel?* for both 'how much?' and 'how many?'

MY/YOUR

Instead of *der/die/das* (the) or *ein/eine/ein* (a) you may want to use the possessive *mein* (m.)/*meine* (f.)/*mein* (n.), meaning 'my', or *Ihr* (m.)/*Ihre* (f.)/*Ihr* (n.), meaning 'your'.

wie ist | *Ihr Name* (m.)?
| *Ihre Zimmernummer* (f.)?

wie groß ist Ihr Zelt (n.)?

mein Name (m.) *ist Bessen*

meine Zimmernummer (f.) *ist 75*

mein Zelt (n.) *ist ein Zweipersonenzelt*

You may have noticed other endings on words like *ein, mein, Ihr:*

darf ich meinen Schlüssel bitte haben?

ich bin hier mit meinem Wohnwagen

After most verbs you use *den, meinen, Ihren,* etc. with masculine nouns (i.e. when they're the direct object).

But don't worry if you get the endings wrong. You'll still be understood.

PLURALS

In English you say 'one room' but 'two rooms', 'one child' but 'two children', 'one loaf' but 'two loaves', 'one sheep' or 'two sheep', and so on. There are a number of different ways of forming plurals in German, too. The noun may add an ending or an *Umlaut* or both. Or it may not change at all. The best way of getting plurals right is to learn them as you go along. In the word list at the end of the book what you add to make a noun plural is given in brackets, like this:

SINGULAR	PLURAL
die Woche (-n)	*die Wochen*
das Hotel (-s)	*die Hotels*
der Tag (-e)	*die Tage*
die Nacht (-̈e)	*die Nächte*
das Kind (-er)	*die Kinder*
das Zimmer (-)	*die Zimmer*

With all plural nouns the word for 'the' is *die,* 'my' is *meine* and 'your' is *Ihre*.

BITTE SCHÖN

In German you'll hear *bitte* or *bitte schön* or *bitte sehr* all the time. You say it if someone thanks you, in the sense of 'not at all'. You also say it when you're handing someone something or doing them some kind of service, opening the door perhaps, or passing them something at the table. Then it means something like 'there you are'.

AUF WIEDERHÖREN!

On the phone you don't say *auf Wiedersehen* (*lit.* until we see each other again) but *auf Wiederhören* (until we hear each other again). But that may change with the introduction of picture-phones!

EXERCISES

TELEPHONING A HOTEL

1 At the station you see a free hotel telephone. You decide to
try to get a room at the Hotel zur Post.

EMPFANG   *(answering the phone)* Hotel zur Post, guten
            Tag. Bitte schön?

SIE   (Say good day, and tell her you'd like a single
            room with a shower.)

EMPFANG   Ja, sicherlich, das haben wir.

SIE   (Inquire about the price.)

EMPFANG   Das kostet hundertfünf Mark pro Nacht.

SIE   (Oh! Don't accept.)

EMPFANG   Schade! Tut mir leid. Auf Wiederhören.

AT THE TOURIST INFORMATION CENTER

2 After that you decide to go to the tourist information center
and ask for a room there. What do you say?

ANGESTELLTE   Guten Tag. Was kann ich für Sie tun?

SIE   (You'd like to reserve a room.)

ANGESTELLTE   Ja, gern. Was für ein Zimmer möchten Sie?

SIE   (A single room with a shower.)

ANGESTELLTE   Und für wie viele Nächte möchten Sie
              bleiben?

SIE   (Four nights, please.)

ANGESTELLTE   Ich kann Ihnen ein sehr schönes Zimmer im
              Palast Hotel anbieten.

SIE   (Inquire about the price.)

ANGESTELLTE   Das Zimmer kostet achtzig Mark pro Nacht.

SIE   (Accept.)

CHECKING IN

3 You arrive at the Palast Hotel and check in. As you're in a hurry to get to an appointment you ask for a taxi right away.

EMPFANG	Guten Tag. Bitte sehr?
SIE	(Introduce yourself, and say you've reserved a room.)
EMPFANG	Ja, richtig. Ein Einzelzimmer für vier Nächte. Möchten Sie ein Zimmer mit Bad oder mit Dusche?
SIE	(With a shower.)
EMPFANG	Gut. Dürfte ich Sie bitten, sich einzutragen?
SIE	(Hand back the form.)
EMPFANG	Danke sehr. Hier ist Ihr Schlüssel. Zimmer hundertsiebzehn in der ersten Etage. Kann ich sonst noch etwas für Sie tun?
SIE	(Ask if she can call you a taxi.)
EMPFANG	Ja, sicher. *(phones for a taxi)* Es kommt gleich.
SIE	(Thank her.)

ROOM SERVICE

4 Back in your room you'd like a drink. You call reception.

EMPFANG	*(answering the phone)* Empfang. Bitte sehr?
SIE	(You'd like a bottle of wine.)
EMPFANG	Gern. Roten oder weißen?
SIE	(White, please.)
EMPFANG	Darf es sonst noch etwas sein?
SIE	(Yes, a bottle of mineral water, please.)
EMPFANG	Vielen Dank. Kommt sofort. Wiederhören.
SIE	(Thank you and goodbye.)

AT THE CAMPGROUND

5 Traveling by car and with a tent you've arrived at a campground. What do you say to the manager?

PLATZWART	Guten Tag, die Herrschaften. Was kann ich für Sie tun?
SIE	(Ask if he still has tent sites available.)
PLATZWART	Ja, sicherlich. Wie viele Personen sind Sie?
SIE	(You're three adults and a child.)
PLATZWART	Haben Sie ein Fahrzeug?
SIE	(Answer and ask the price.)
PLATZWART	Die Erwachsenen kosten sechs Mark, das Kind kostet vier Mark, und das Auto kostet dreizehn Mark fünfzig pro Nacht.
SIE	(Accept.)

WORTH KNOWING

HOTELS

In Germany there are no official hotel categories, but hotels
often give themselves unofficial ratings ranging from one to
five stars, and 'luxury' for the very best.

Hamburg's most famous hotel is the *Vier Jahreszeiten,* listed
among the world's ten leading Grand Hotels. Situated directly
on the *Binnenalster,* it's ideal for an after-shopping snack or a
meal in one of its two superb restaurants.

TOURIST INFORMATION

A tourist information center can be found in almost every
town, often in or near the town hall. It's often called *der
Verkehrsverein* or *der Fremdenverkehrsverein* but you can usually

recognize it by the international sign 'i' (for *Information*). You can reserve accommodations via the tourist information center although – especially when you're on vacation and have the time – you might be better advised to have a look around the hotels yourself first, to find the place that suits you best.

Tourist information centers can give you plenty of advice about what to see and do and they often sell theater or concert tickets as well.

REGISTRATION

By law everybody staying in any kind of public accommodation is required to register. Information about guests (name, home address, signature) is routinely given to the police.

CAMPING

You can find campgrounds for motor homes or tents all over Germany. Standards and prices vary considerably and it's a good idea to inquire before traveling. Advance reservations are often necessary, especially during the vacation season. For further information contact the ADAC (*Allgemeiner Deutscher Automobil-Club,* the German automobile association) near your destination or as soon as you enter the country.

4 GETTING ABOUT

KEY WORDS AND PHRASES

FINDING OUT WHERE PLACES ARE

wo ist . . . ?	where is . . . ?
(wo) gibt es . . . ?	(where) is there . . . ?
hier in der Nähe?	near here?

. . . AND HOW TO GET THERE

wie komme ich . . .	how do I get . . .
zum Jungfernstieg?	to the Jungfernstieg?
zur Autobahn?	to the expressway
nach Bremen?	to Bremen?

SOME KEY DIRECTIONS

Sie gehen	you go
Sie fahren	you drive
rechts	on/to the right
links	on/to the left
geradeaus	straight ahead
um die Ecke	round the corner
über (die Brücke)	across (the bridge)
die nächste/erste/zweite Straße	the next/first/second street
auf der rechten/linken Seite	on the right-hand/left-hand side

TRAVELING BY TRAIN

einmal/zweimal	one/two tickets (once/twice)
erster zweiter Klasse	first/second class
einfache Fahrt	one way
hin und zurück	round trip

CONVERSATIONS

ASKING DIRECTIONS

Excuse me, where's the nearest bus stop?

FR. HARRINGTON Entschuldigen Sie bitte, wo ist die nächste Bushaltestelle?

FRAU RADTKE Die nächste Bushaltestelle ist gleich hier nebenan, um die nächste Ecke. Da fährt der Bus ab.

Where's the art gallery, please? Is it far?

FRAU PAGITZ Wo ist die Kunsthalle, bitte?

FRAU HERBST Sie gehen bitte die nächste Straße rechts hinunter, links über die Brücke, und dann sehen Sie direkt das Gebäude.

FRAU PAGITZ Ist das weit?

FRAU HERBST Das ist ungefähr zwei Minuten zu Fuß.

FRAU PAGITZ Ah, wunderbar. Danke schön.

Is there a pharmacy nearby? I'm a stranger here.

HERR HINZE Entschuldigen Sie bitte, gibt es hier in der Nähe eine Apotheke?

FRAU HERBST Ja, natürlich. Die Hauptbahnhofapotheke. Die ist direkt über den Hachmannplatz hinüber auf der rechten Seite.

HERR HINZE Und wo ist der Hachmannplatz? Ich bin fremd hier.

FRAU HERBST	Direkt hier vor dem Haus.
HERR HINZE	Ah, danke schön.
FRAU HERBST	Bitte.

Where's there a supermarket near here?

FRAU HADRIAN	Wo gibt es hier einen Supermarkt?
BEAMTER	Wenn Sie diese Straße entlang gehen etwa fünf Minuten, dann finden Sie ihn auf der rechten Seite.
FRAU HADRIAN	Danke schön.

What's the best way to the Jungfernstieg? I'd like to walk.

HERR KOTHE	Entschuldigen Sie bitte, wie komme ich am besten zum Jungfernstieg?
FRAU KRÜGER	Möchten Sie zu Fuß gehen?
HERR KOTHE	Ja, ich möchte zu Fuß gehen.
FRAU KRÜGER	Da gehen Sie einfach hier links, geradeaus immer an der Alster lang. Da kommen Sie automatisch zum Jungfernstieg.
HERR KOTHE	Und wie weit ist das?
FRAU KRÜGER	Zu Fuß zirka fünfzehn Minuten.

How do I get to the Bremen expressway? Ah, it's marked with road signs.

FR. HARRINGTON	Wie komme ich zur Autobahn nach Bremen?
HERR HINZE	Oh, da muß ich einen Moment überlegen. Sie fahren hier weiter geradeaus, dann die zweite links. Und dann ist es die erste wieder rechts. Und da ist ein Schild 'Autobahn Bremen'.
FR. HARRINGTON	Ach, es ist ausgeschildert.
HERR HINZE	Ja.
FR. HARRINGTON	Das ist ja gut.

What's the quickest way to the Ost-West-Straße? *Is it very far from here?*

DR. GÖTTSCH — Wie komme ich denn am schnellsten zur Ost-West-Straße?

FRAU PETERS — Das ist ganz einfach von hier. Sie sind jetzt beim alten Elbtunnel, da fahren Sie geradeaus bis zur nächsten Ampel und biegen nach links in die Helgoländer Allee ein. Da fahren Sie bis zum Millerntorplatz weiter und dann rechts in die Ost-West-Straße.

DR. GÖTTSCH — Ist es sehr weit von hier?

FRAU PETERS — Ach, nur ein paar Minuten.

AROUND THE CITY

At the hairdresser's. What are your opening hours?

FR. HARRINGTON — Wie sind Ihre Öffnungszeiten?

FRAU RADTKE — Wir haben von Montag bis Freitag von acht Uhr dreißig bis achtzehn Uhr geöffnet, und sonnabends von acht bis zwölf Uhr.

At the Tourist Information Center. I'd like to go on a city tour. When does the next one leave?

HERR HINZE — Ich möchte gerne eine Stadtrundfahrt machen. Wann geht denn die nächste?

FRAU HERBST — Die nächste Stadtrundfahrt ist um vierzehn Uhr.

HERR HINZE — Und was kostet die?

FRAU HERBST — Pro Person zweiundzwanzig Mark.

HERR HINZE — Ja, dann hätte ich gern zwei Karten.

Booking a trip around Hamburg harbor. Two adults, please. How long does the trip last?

HR. BRINKMANN — Hafenrundfahrt hier! Hier die Abfahrt! Wollen Sie auch noch mit? Hier gleich eine

Abfahrt! Einsteigen, mitreisen! Hafenrundfahrt hier!

FRAU EVRAHR   Guten Tag. Zwei Erwachsene, bitte.

HR. BRINKMANN   Zwei Erwachsene, à Person zwölf Mark,
vierundzwanzig Mark, bitte.

FRAU EVRAHR   Wie lange dauert die Fahrt?

HR. BRINKMANN   Eine gute Stunde.

BUS AND TRAIN

What number (bus) goes downtown?

FR. HARRINGTON   Welche Nummer fährt in die Innenstadt?

FRAU RADTKE   Der Hundertsiebenundfünfziger.

FR. HARRINGTON   Vielen Dank.

*At the station. One second-class ticket to Würzburg,
please. Round-trip.*

HERR KOTHE   Einmal zweiter Klasse nach Würzburg, bitte.

BEAMTER   Einfache Fahrt oder hin und zurück?

HERR KOTHE   Hin und zurück, bitte.

BEAMTER   Einen Moment, bitte.

WORD LIST

gleich hier nebenan	just near here, close by
fährt ab	leaves
die nächste Straße hinunter	down the next street
sehen	to see
direkt	direct(ly), right in front of you
das Gebäude	building
ist das weit?	is that far?
ungefähr zwei Minuten	about two minutes
zu Fuß	on foot
wunderbar	wonderful
natürlich	of course

der **Hauptbahnhof**	main railroad station
vor	in front of
wenn	if
diese Straße entlang	along this street
etwa = ungefähr	about
finden	to find
der Jungfernstieg	street in Hamburg (*lit.* 'path of the virgins')
einfach	simple, simply
dann kommen Sie zu . . .	then you'll come to . . .
automatisch	automatically
zirka = ungefähr	about
ich muß überlegen	I must think
das Schild	sign
das ist ganz einfach	that's quite simple
bis zur (nächsten Ampel)	up to the (next traffic light)
einbiegen in	to turn into
weiter	(farther) on
geöffnet	open
geschlossen	closed
von . . . bis	from . . . to (until)
die (Fahr)karte	ticket
die Abfahrt	departure
wollen Sie auch noch mit?	do you want to come as well?
einsteigen	to board
eine gute Stunde	a good hour

EXPLANATIONS

ASKING WHERE PLACES ARE

wo ist | *der Bahnhof* (m.)?
die Kunsthalle (f.)?
das Hotel Bellevue (n.)?

(wo) gibt es hier	*einen Supermarkt* (m.)?
	eine Apotheke (f.)?
	ein Postamt (n.)? (post office)

With a masculine noun, after *gibt es* you use *einen*.

FINDING OUT HOW TO GET THERE

wie komme ich . . .

	zum Jungfernstieg (m.) ?
am besten	*zur Autobahn* (f.) ?
am schnellsten	*zum Hotel Bellevue* (n.) ?
	nach Bremen?

Notice that with a masculine or neuter noun you use *zum (= zu dem)*, with a feminine noun *zur (=zu der)* and with names of towns (and most countries) *nach*.

GEHEN OR *FAHREN*?

Gehen and *fahren* both mean 'to go.' You use *gehen* when walking is involved, but to travel by any means of transportation is *fahren*. So it's:

mit dem Bus	
mit dem Taxi	
mit dem Zug (train)	*fahren*
mit dem Auto	
mit dem Fahrrad	
mit der Straßenbahn	

But: *zu Fuß gehen*

FIRST, SECOND, THIRD, ETC.

Numbers between 1 and 19 mostly add '. . . *te*':

zwei   *der zweite* (second)

fünf   *der fünfte* (fifth)
zehn   *der zehnte* (tenth)
dreizehn *der dreizehnte* (thirteenth)
But note these:
eins *der erste* (first)
drei *der dritte* (third)

Numbers from 20 onwards add '. . . *ste*':
zweiundzwanzig – *der zweiundzwanzigste* (twenty-second)
neunundvierzig –   *der neunundvierzigste* (forty-ninth)

Written as figures (for example in dates) these endings are
indicated by a period:
22. April – *der zweiundzwanzigste April*
3. September – *der dritte September*

DAYS OF THE WEEK

SEPTEMBER	WOCHE 39
MONTAG 23 *THEATER (LOHENGRIN)*	
DIENSTAG 24 *DR. MÜLLER (ZAHNARZT)* *HAUPTBAHNHOF (PETER ABHOLEN)*	
MITTWOCH 25 *ALSTERPAVILLON MIT SUSANNE*	
DONNERSTAG 26 *FRISEUR!* *SKAT IN DER "GLOCKE"*	
FREITAG 27 *MITTAGESSEN IM HOTEL* *BELLEVUE MIT BARBARA*	
SAMSTAG 28 *MARKT!*	
SONNTAG 29 *OMA*	

Particularly in North Germany, people often say *Sonnabend*
instead of *Samstag*.

TIME

To find out the time, ask: *wieviel Uhr ist es?* To tell someone the time, start with: *es ist . . .* 'Past' is *nach* and 'to' is *vor:*

Es ist
| *neun Uhr* (9 o'clock)
| *fünf nach neun* (five past . . .)
| *Viertel nach neun* (quarter past . . .)
| *Viertel vor zehn* (quarter to . . .)
| *zehn vor zehn* (ten to . . .)

But be careful with 'half past'! Germans think of the hour ahead. 'Half past six' is 'half way to seven', *halb sieben.* 'Half past ten' is 'half way to eleven', *halb elf.*

In official situations, and often in ordinary conversation as well, people use the 24-hour clock:
es ist sechzehn Uhr zwanzig
es ist zweiundzwanzig Uhr fünfundvierzig

'At' a time is *um:*
die nächste Stadtrundfahrt ist um vierzehn Uhr

And 'from . . . to . . .' is *von . . . bis . . . :*
wir haben von acht Uhr dreißig bis achtzehn Uhr geöffnet

BUYING TRAIN TICKETS

You need to say:
how many tickets: *einmal, zweimal, . . .*
first or second class: *erster oder zweiter Klasse*
one-way or round-trip: *einfach oder hin und zurück*
where you're going: *nach Bremen*

EXERCISES

GOING BY SUBWAY

1   It's your first morning in Hamburg and you want to explore the city. At the hotel reception desk you ask where the nearest subway station is:

SIE   _____?

EMPFANG   Die nächste U–Bahn Station ist zwei Straßen weiter, gleich links um die Ecke.

2   At the subway station you inquire which number goes downtown.

SIE   _____?

MANN   Die U 3 fährt in die Innenstadt.

FINDING A CAFÉ

3   After some sightseeing you feel like having coffee. You stop a passer-by and ask if there's a café nearby.

SIE   _____?

PASSANT   Ja, sicher. Sie gehen über die Alsterallee, biegen links in die erste Straße und gehen immer geradeaus. Dann die zweite Straße rechts gehen Sie bis zur Hamburger Straße. Direkt links an der Ecke ist ein schönes Café.

SIE   (Inquire if it's far.)

PASSANT   Nein. Nur ungefähr zehn Minuten zu Fuß.

4   As you've got a city map *(overleaf)* you mark in the position of the café:

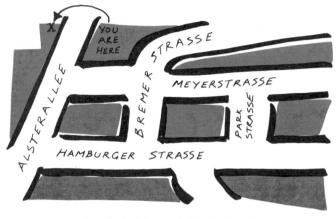

WHEN IS THE BANK OPEN?

5 On the way to the café you pass a bank. You go in to inquire about opening hours.

SIE _____ ?

ANGESTELLTER Wir haben von Montag bis Mittwoch von neun bis sechzehn Uhr dreißig geöffnet, am Donnerstag von neun bis achtzehn Uhr und am Freitag von neun bis vierzehn Uhr dreißig.

SIE (Ask if they're open on Saturdays.)

ANGESTELLTER Sonnabends haben wir nicht geöffnet.

6 Did you understand the times? See if you can complete the notice:

DEUTSCHE BANK, HAMBURG		
ÖFFNUNGSZEITEN :		
Mo./Di./Mi.:	_____ Uhr bis	_____ Uhr
Donnerstag:	_____ Uhr bis	_____ Uhr
Freitag:	_____ Uhr bis	_____ Uhr
Samstag:	_____	

WHICH SIGHTSEEING TRIP?

7   Seeing the tourist information center you decide to go on a sightseeing tour. You enjoy boat trips, it's Tuesday and about 2 p.m., you have to be back at your hotel by 5:30 p.m., and it takes you about 45 minutes to get there. Which of these trips do you choose?

HAMBURG SEHEN UND LIEBEN!

Unsere Rundfahrten geben Ihnen den besten Eindruck:

Große Stadtrundfahrt mit Hafenrundfahrt
täglich 10 und 14 Uhr
Dauer etwa 3 Stunden

Große Stadtrundfahrt
täglich 11, 13 and 15 Uhr
Dauer ca. 2 Stunden

Große Hafenrundfahrt
Mittwoch, Sonnabend und Sonntag jeweils 11 und 15 Uhr
Dauer ca. 1¼ Stunde

Kleine Stadtrundfahrt mit Alster-Bootsfahrt
täglich 10.30, 14.30 und 16 Uhr
Dauer ca. 2 Stunden

Kombinierte Hafenrundfahrt und Alsterfahrt
Dienstag, Donnerstag, Samstag 12 und 15 Uhr
Dauer ca. 2½ Stunden

WORTH KNOWING

PUBLIC TRANSPORTATION

Bus and streetcar stops in Germany are indicated by a green H (for *Haltestelle*) in a green circle on a yellow background. Subway systems are indicated by the familiar U (for *Untergrundbahn*) and the fast local railway system by S (for *Schnellbahn*). Often you can use the same ticket on all of them, but it's wise to check if you don't want to be caught with an invalid ticket by the ticket inspector.

Waiting in line (unfortunately) isn't a German habit, and everybody just pushes forward as soon as the vehicle arrives.

You can buy bus and streetcar tickets in advance from slot machines or tobacco shops. If you don't have a ticket, get in the front car as they are only available from the driver. For the subway or *S-Bahn* you also have to get a ticket in advance, usually from a slot machine at the station.

BUYING MEDICINES

In Germany only pharmacies *(Apotheken)* sell drugs, though a few, mainly 'natural', medicines may be bought at drugstores *(Drogerien)* or in supermarkets.

There are always a number of pharmacies open at night for emergencies. You'll find a list on display at any pharmacy in town.

GERMAN RAILWAYS

The *Deutsche Bundesbahn* – still the *Deutsche Reichsbahn* in eastern parts – provides an excellent service throughout the country. Rapid *InterCity (IC)* trains connect all important cities every hour, while *EuroCity (EC)* trains run direct into neighboring countries. To get you there even sooner, new tracks are currently under construction for these fast services and for *InterCity Expreß (ICE)* trains. When traveling InterCity or EuroCity you have to pay a supplement *(der Zuschlag)*.

FD-Züge or *Fernschnellzüge* (long-distance expresses) and *D-Züge* or *Schnellzüge* (ordinary expresses) also link major cities (a supplement is usually required for journeys under 50 km). More local services are provided by Inter-Regio, *E-Züge* or *Eilzüge* (fast trains), and *Personenzüge* (slow trains).

MORE ABOUT TIME

Germans sometimes count minutes to or past the half hour (often between twenty minutes past and twenty minutes to the hour):

25 past 3   *fünf vor halb vier*
              (five minutes to half past three)
27 minutes to 8 *drei nach halb acht*
              (three minutes past half past seven)

You needn't use this way of saying the time yourself, but understanding it could be useful.

5 EATING OUT

ORDERING

die Speisekarte, bitte	the menu, please
die Scholle, bitte	the plaice, please
ich nehme . . .	I'll have . . .
für mich . . .	for me . . .
das Zitronensorbet	the lemon sorbet
einen trockenen Sherry	a dry sherry

THE WAITER MAY ASK:

haben Sie schon gewählt?	have you chosen?
hat es Ihnen geschmeckt?	did you enjoy it?
darf ich Ihnen noch etwas anbieten?	may I offer you anything else?
guten Appetit!	enjoy your meal!

CONVERSATIONS

BREAKFAST, COFFEE, TEA, CAKES

Breakfast at the Hotel Bellevue. Coffee, please.

OBER   Guten Morgen, der Herr. Möchten Sie
           Kaffee, Tee . . . ?

HERR KOTHE	Kaffee, bitte.
OBER	Ja, bring' ich Ihnen sofort. Wir haben ein Frühstücksbüffet, möchten Sie sich daran bedienen?
HERR KOTHE	Ja, gern.

At the Alsterpavillon. *Two pots of coffee. And a piece of apple strudel, please. With cream.*

OBER	Ja, bitte?
FRAU EVRAHR	Bitte zwei Kännchen Kaffee, und für mich ein Stück Nußtorte.
OBER	*(to Herr Knuth)* Und für Sie, bitte?
HERR KNUTH	Ein Stück Apfelstrudel, bitte.
OBER	Den Apfelstrudel mit Sahne oder ohne Sahne?
HERR KNUTH	Mit Sahne.

At a café. A glass of tea. May I have your 'cake ticket', please?

KELLNERIN	Guten Tag. Bitte schön?
KUNDIN	Ich hätte gerne ein Glas Tee.
KELLNERIN	Ja, gerne. Bekommen Sie auch Kuchen?
KUNDIN	Ja, ich hab' ein Stück Himbeertorte bestellt.
KELLNERIN	Dann geben Sie mir bitte Ihren Kuchenbon.
KUNDIN	Bitte schön.

DINNER AT THE HOTEL

Here's the menu. Would you like an aperitif first?

OBER	Guten Tag, der Herr. Möchten Sie speisen?
HERR KOTHE	Ja, bitte.
OBER	Hier, die Speisekarte für Sie.
HERR KOTHE	Vielen Dank.
OBER	Möchten Sie vorab einen Aperitif trinken?
HERR KOTHE	Ja . . . ich nehme einen trockenen Sherry, bitte.

*First I'd like the Hamburg crayfish soup. Then the
plaice, please. And a Franconian wine, a nice dry one.*

OBER	Der Herr, haben Sie schon gewählt?
HERR KOTHE	Ja, als Vorspeise hätte ich gern die Hamburger Krebssuppe.
OBER	Und als Hauptgang?
HERR KOTHE	Die Scholle, bitte.
OBER	Ja. Und Sie trinken dazu?
HERR KOTHE	Einen Frankenwein, glaub' ich.
OBER	Einen schönen trockenen Frankenwein?
HERR KOTHE	Ja, bitte.

It was excellent. I'll have the lemon sorbet, please.

OBER	So, der Herr, hat's Ihnen geschmeckt?
HERR KOTHE	Ja, ausgezeichnet. Danke.
OBER	Darf ich Ihnen noch etwas anbieten? Ein kleines Dessert?
HERR KOTHE	Ja, ich nehm' das Zitronensorbet Bellevue, bitte.
OBER	Ja, kommt sofort.

Put the meal on my bill, please.

HERR KOTHE	Herr Ober, schreiben Sie das Essen bitte mit auf meine Rechnung.
OBER	Welche Zimmernummer haben Sie?
HERR KOTHE	Nummer fünfundsiebzig.
OBER	Kleinen Moment, bitte . . . *(he brings the check)* Bitte schön, ich brauch' eine Unterschrift.

AT THE RESTAURANT

In the restaurant Überseebrücke. *What's the soup of the
day?*

FR. HARRINGTON	Die Tagessuppe, was ist das heute?
OBER	Das ist eine Hamburger Krabbensuppe.

FR. HARRINGTON	Das klingt gut. Die möcht' ich gern.
OBER	Ja, gerne.

In the restaurant Schifferbörse. *What would you recommend today?*

HERR HINZE	Was würden Sie uns denn heute empfehlen?
OBER	Möchten Sie Fisch oder Fleisch?
FRAU EVRAHR	Also, ich nehme gerne Fisch.
OBER	Da hab' ich ein sehr schönes Heilbuttsteak, gebraten, mit Zitronenbutter, Kopfsalat und Dillkartoffeln.
FRAU EVRAHR	Das nehme ich.
OBER	Gerne. Und für den Herrn, bitte?
HERR HINZE	Ich hätte gerne Fleisch.
OBER	Ja, da hab' ich einen sehr schönen Schifferbörsentopf.
HERR HINZE	Was ist das, bitte?
OBER	Das sind drei verschiedene Filets.
HERR HINZE	Mit frischem Gemüse, Champignons, auf Bratkartoffeln.
OBER	Ja.
HERR HINZE	Aha, dann möchte ich gerne den Schifferbörsentopf.

Enjoy your meal! Guten Appetit!

OBER	Ich wünsch' Ihnen einen guten Appetit.
FRAU EVRAHR	Vielen Dank.
OBER	Bitte.
HERR HINZE	*(to Frau Evrahr)* Ja, guten Appetit!
FRAU EVRAHR	Ja, danke. Gleichfalls.

The check, please! Keep the change!

HERR HINZE	Herr Ober! Die Rechnung, bitte.
OBER	Ja, ich mach' Ihnen gleich die Rechnung fertig . . . *(bringing the check)* Bitte schön.
HERR HINZE	Danke. Einen Moment. Bitte . . . *(puts the*

money and a tip on the plate) So, das stimmt
so. Danke.

OBER   Ja. Vielen Dank.

WORD LIST

für mich	for me
der Herr	sir
die Dame	madam
das Frühstücksbüffet	breakfast buffet
sich daran bedienen	help yourself from it
bekommen Sie auch Kuchen?	are you having cake as well?
ich habe . . . bestellt	I've ordered . . .
die Himbeertorte	raspberry tart
geben Sie mir . . .	give me . . .
speisen	to eat, dine
vorab	to begin with
der Hauptgang	main course
und Sie trinken dazu?	and to drink with it?
glaube ich	I think
ich brauche . . .	I need . . .
der Fisch	fish
das Fleisch	meat
das Heilbuttsteak	halibut steak
gebraten	fried
der Kopfsalat	lettuce
die Dillkartoffeln (f. pl.)	potatoes with dill
verschieden	different
mit frischem Gemüse	with fresh vegetables
die Champignons (m. pl.)	mushrooms
die Bratkartoffeln (f. pl.)	fried potatoes
gleichfalls	the same to you
ich mache Ihnen . . . fertig	I'll prepare . . . for you

EXPLANATIONS

GETTING THE MENU

Ask for: *die Speisekarte, bitte.* Don't confuse it with *das Menü!*
Ein Menü is a fixed-price set meal. If you want a drink with
your meal, ask for *die Weinkarte* or *die Getränkekarte.*

ORDERING

As with asking for things in shops, you can just say what you
want and add *bitte.* Or you can start with *ich möchte* or *ich hätte
gern* (I'd like) or *ich nehme* (I'll have):
ein Stück Apfelstrudel, bitte
ich hätte gern ein Glas Tee
ich möchte den Schifferbörsentopf
ich nehme einen trockenen Sherry
If what you order is a masculine word, you use *einen* or *den.*

For me and for you:
für mich ein Stück Nußtorte. Und für Sie?
To say what you'd like for a particular course use *als:*
als Vorspeise hätte ich gern die Hamburger Krebssuppe
als Hauptgang, die Scholle, bitte
als Dessert nehme ich das Zitronensorbet
Asking for a recommendation:
was würden Sie heute empfehlen?
To find out what something is:
was ist das?

You'll need to understand what the waiter says. He may ask:
. . . what you'd like:

	speisen?
möchten Sie	*vorab einen Aperitif trinken?*
	Fisch oder Fleisch?

. . . if you've made your choice:
haben Sie schon gewählt?
. . . whether you enjoyed it:
hat's Ihnen geschmeckt?
. . . if he can offer you anything else:
darf ich Ihnen noch etwas anbieten?
And he's almost sure to wish you:
guten Appetit!

SETTLING THE CHECK

Asking for the check: *die Rechnung, bitte!*
And you'll probably want to give a tip:
stimmt so! or *das ist für Sie*

ABOUT WORD ORDER

In a simple German sentence the verb is the second element
(though not necessarily the second word):
ich/nehme/gern Fleisch
als Vorspeise/hätte/ich gern die Hamburger Krebssuppe
da/hab'/ich ein sehr schönes Heilbuttsteak

The verb is also the second element in a question beginning
with a question word:
was/ist/das?
welche Zimmernummer/haben/Sie?

If there's no specific question word, the question usually starts
with a verb:
bekommen/Sie auch Kuchen?
möchten/Sie speisen?
haben/Sie schon gewählt?

EXERCISES

SORTING OUT THE MENU

Here are some headings and items you might find on the menu. Which dishes in the right-hand column belong to which headings on the left?

1 Fleisch   **a** Frische Nordsee-Scholle
2 Getränke   **b** Ungarische Gulaschsuppe
3 Desserts   **c** Rumpsteak vom Grill
4 Warme u. kalte Vorspeisen   **d** Rheinwein
5 Suppen   **e** Krabbencocktail
6 Fischspezialitäten   **f** Vanille-Eis mit heißer
                                     Schokolade

ORDERING A MEAL

7 You're eating out and this is the menu *(overleaf)*.

OBER   Guten Tag, die Dame/der Herr. Haben Sie schon gewählt?
SIE   (Order the Hamburg fish soup with garlic bread.)
OBER   Ja, gern. Und als Hauptgericht?
SIE   (As a main course you'll have North Sea plaice with Büsum★ prawns and parsley potatoes.)
OBER   Was trinken Sie dazu, bitte?
SIE   (You'd like a Rhine wine.)
OBER   Sehr gern. Haben Sie schon ein Dessert gewählt?
SIE   (Yes. Hot raspberries with vanilla ice cream and cream, please.)
OBER   Vielen Dank.

★Büsum: resort and fishing center on the North Sea coast, north of the Elbe.

Restaurant im Keller

Speisekarte

KALTE UND WARME VORSPEISEN
Knackfrischer Salat 6,50 DM
Forellenfilet mit Sahnemeerrettich, Toast und Butter 8,50 DM
Krabbencocktail 17,50 DM

SUPPEN
Tagessuppe 6,50 DM   Hamburger Krabbensuppe 8,50 DM
Ungarische Gulaschsuppe 7,50 DM   Hamburger Fischsuppe mit Knoblauchbrot 9,00 DM

FISCH
Schollenfilet mit Champignons, Artischocken und Butterkartoffeln 19,50 DM
Nordseescholle mit Büsumer Krabben und Petersilienkartoffeln 26,50 DM
Lachssteak vom Grill mit Tomaten, Champignons und Dillkartoffeln 29,50 DM
Seezungenfilet mit zerlassener Butter, Salzkartoffeln und Salatteller 41,50 DM

FLEISCH
Hamburger Labskaus, pikante Beilagen 16,50 DM
Lammfilets auf Knoblauchsauce, Blattspinat und Butterkartoffeln 21,50 DM
Kapitänspfanne mit drei kleinen Steaks, frischem Gemüse und Butterkartoffeln 23,50 DM
Pfeffersteak mit Petersilienkartoffeln und Salaten der Saison 36,50 DM

DESSERTS
Gemischtes Eis mit Sahne 6,50 DM   Eiscafé mit Sahne 6,50 DM
Heiße Himbeeren mit Vanille-Eis und Sahne 9,50 DM

SCHOPPENWEINE

Rhein 0,2l 7,50 DM		*Rotwein 0,2l 7,50 DM*
Mosel 0,2l 7,50 DM	*Franken 0,2l 9,50 DM*	*Rosé 0,2l 7,50 DM*

Preise verstehen sich incl. Bedienung und Mehrwertsteuer

PAYING BY CREDIT CARD

8   You've finished your meal and want to pay by credit card.

OBER	Hat es Ihnen geschmeckt?
SIE	(You found it excellent. And ask for the check.)
OBER	Ja, gerne. Ich mache Ihnen sofort die Rechnung fertig.
SIE	(You want to pay, *bezahlen,* by credit card.)
OBER	Ja, gerne. Bitte, einen Moment . . . *(takes the card, returns with the slip)* Darf ich Sie bitten, hier zu unterschreiben?
SIE	(Yes, certainly. And give him a tip, saying, 'And that's for you.')
OBER	Vielen Dank. Auf Wiedersehen.
SIE	(Goodbye.)

9   Make out the check by copying from the menu the dishes
you had with their prices. What does that come to – in German?

COFFEE AND CAKE

10   Later you go to a café for *Kaffee und Kuchen*.

OBER	Ja, bitte?
SIE	(Coffee and a piece of lemon cake, please.)
OBER	Ein Kännchen oder eine Tasse Kaffee?
SIE	(A cup, please.)
OBER	Und die Zitronentorte mit oder ohne Sahne?
SIE	(With cream.)
OBER	Gerne. Kommt sofort.

WORTH KNOWING

BREAKFAST

In hotels a set breakfast usually consists of various kinds of
bread, rolls and preserves, sliced cheese, cold meats and
sausage and perhaps a boiled egg (though many hotels now
offer a breakfast of your choice from a breakfast buffet).
Breakfast may or may not be included in the room price. To
find out, ask: *ist das mit Frühstück?*

A GLASS OF TEA, A CUP OF COFFEE

As mentioned earlier, tea in a German restaurant or café can
be quite expensive. So, instead of a pot, people often order
just a glass. (There's even a special size of teabag, *die
Glasportion*.) You'll never get a single *cup* of tea in a German
restaurant, but you can order a cup of coffee. Restaurants
sometimes refuse to serve a single glass of tea or a single cup

of coffee on weekends or holidays, or outside on the terrace.
Then you have to order a – more expensive – pot.

'CAKE TICKETS'

Most cafés display their pastries and cakes at a glass-covered
counter, from which you make your choice. The counter
assistant will give you one part of a numbered voucher, rather
like a hatcheck ticket. The other half goes onto the plate with
the cake you've chosen. The waitress at the table will collect
your half of the ticket and serve the matching cake together
with your drink.

HAMBURGER KREBSSUPPE

Many towns and cities have their own local specialties. In
Hamburg these include *Hamburger Krebssuppe* (crayfish soup)
and *Hamburger Aalsuppe* (eel soup). If you prefer something
more substantial, try *Finkenwerder Ewerscholle,* locally caught
plaice served with bacon, or *Labskaus,* a traditional sailor's
dish made from mashed potatoes with corned beef, herring,
beets, and a fried egg.

CALLING THE WAITER OR WAITRESS

Calling a waiter is easy. Just say: *Herr Ober!* In a bar – and if
you're sure he's the proprietor himself – you can call him:
Herr Wirt.

It used to be customary to call the waitress *Fräulein,* but today
waitresses increasingly resent this form of address, which was
originally used only for unmarried women. So, to be on the
safe side, just say: *Hallo!* Or indicate with your hand that
you want her attention.

GUTEN APPETIT!

People will wish you *guten Appetit!* both in restaurants and at family meals. Sometimes saying it indicates the official beginning of the meal.

RUHETAG

Most restaurants are closed for one day a week. This is usually indicated by a sign, *Ruhetag* (rest day) on the door.

TIPPING

Although service is included in prices at hotels and restaurants, waiters normally expect about 10 percent of the charge as a tip. You can either hand the waiter the sum including the tip and say: *stimmt so* (that's all right) or, if you have no small change or are paying by credit card, you can simply say how much you want to pay, including tip. For example, with a check of 36,50 DM, you might say: *vierzig Mark*. If you give the tip separately, say: *das ist für Sie* (that's for you), or you can just leave some money on the plate.

6 DOWN TO BUSINESS

KEY WORDS AND PHRASES

PEOPLE'S JOBS

was sind Sie von Beruf?	what's your job?
wo arbeiten Sie?	where do you work?
ich bin Ingenieur	I'm an engineer
ich arbeite bei (der Firma) Siemens	I work at Siemens

ARRANGING A MEETING

geht es . . .	is it possible . . .
morgen früh?	tomorrow morning?
um elf?	at eleven?
am Donnerstag nachmittag?	on Thursday afternoon?
das geht (nicht)	that's (not) possible

ARRIVING FOR AN APPOINTMENT

ich habe um 14 Uhr einen Termin bei Herrn Seel	I've an appointment with Herr Seel at 2 o'clock

TELEPHONING

ich möchte Herrn Gehrels sprechen	I'd like to speak to Herr Gehrels
ich rufe gegen zehn Uhr wieder an	I'll call back again at about ten

SOCIALIZING

sind Sie verheiratet?	are you married?
haben Sie Kinder?	have you got children?
wie heißen sie?	what are their names?
wie alt sind sie?	how old are they?

CONVERSATIONS

The conversations in this chapter were recorded in Hamburg and in other cities.

PEOPLE'S JOBS

In Munich. I'm an engineer. I work at Neuberger Meßinstrumente Ltd.

HR. V. STETTEN	Wie ist Ihr Name, bitte?
HERR HOLZNER	Mein Name ist Gerd Holzner.
HR. V. STETTEN	Und woher kommen Sie?
HERR HOLZNER	Aus München.
HR. V. STETTEN	Was sind Sie von Beruf?
HERR HOLZNER	Ich bin Ingenieur.
HR. V. STETTEN	Und wo arbeiten Sie?
HERR HOLZNER	Ich arbeite bei der Firma Neuberger Meßinstrumente GmbH.

At Polyband, Munich. This is my marketing manager, this is my product manager.

HERR WINKEL	Das ist mein Marketingmanager, Herr Dünker . . .
HERR HUBER	Grüß Gott.
HERR DÜNKER	Herr Huber, grüß Gott.
HERR WINKEL	Und mein Produktmanager, Herr Bergheim.
HERR BERGHEIM	Grüß Gott, Herr Huber.
HERR HUBER	Grüß Gott, Herr Bergheim.

APPOINTMENTS
. . . .

I need a haircut. Preferably tomorrow morning. Is it possible at eleven?

FR. HARRINGTON	Ich brauche einen neuen Haarschnitt, waschen und fönen.
FRAU RADTKE	Wann möchten Sie kommen?
FR. HARRINGTON	Am liebsten morgen früh.
FRAU RADTKE	Um zehn?
FR. HARRINGTON	Geht es auch um elf?
FRAU RADTKE	Es geht auch um elf.
FR. HARRINGTON	Ja, gut. Machen wir das.
FRAU RADTKE	Dann trag' ich Sie um elf Uhr ein.
FR. HARRINGTON	Okay. Bis dann.

At Polyband, Munich. I'd like to have a product meeting on Thursday afternoon. Is that all right with you?

HERR BERGHEIM	Herr Dünker, ich möchte gerne ein Produktmeeting machen, am Donnerstag nachmittag. Geht das bei Ihnen?
HERR DÜNKER	Moment, da muß ich erstmal nachsehen . . . Donnerstag nicht, aber es ginge am Freitag vormittag.
HERR BERGHEIM	Um neun Uhr?
HERR DÜNKER	Um neun Uhr . . . Ja, um neun Uhr ist in Ordnung.

At Audi, Ingolstadt. I've an appointment with Herr Seel at 2 o'clock.

HR. V. STETTEN	Grüß Gott!
PFÖRTNER	Grüß Gott!
HR. V. STETTEN	Mein Name ist von Stetten. Ich komm' aus London. Ich hab' um vierzehn Uhr einen Termin bei Herrn Seel.
PFÖRTNER	Moment, bitte, Herr von Stetten. Ich melde

	Sie an, ja? Moment, bitte.
HR. V. STETTEN	Gut. Danke.

TELEPHONING

At Lufthansa, Hamburg. What's your telephone number? I have a direct line . . . The code for Hamburg is 040.

HERR BESSEN	Wie ist Ihr Name, bitte?
HR. FÜSSINGER	Mein Name ist Peter Füssinger.
HERR BESSEN	Und Ihre Telefonnummer hier in der Firma bei der Lufthansa?
HR. FÜSSINGER	Ich habe eine Durchwahlnummer; die ist fünf null neun zwo fünf sieben drei.
HERR BESSEN	Und die Vorwahlnummer von Hamburg?
HR. FÜSSINGER	Die Vorwahl ist null vier null.

At Pringle, Düsseldorf. Excuse me, what was your name again? And your telephone number?

HR. PERLBACH	Entschuldigung, wie war nochmal Ihr Name?
FRAU PAESCH	Paesch.
HR. PERLBACH	Und Ihre Telefonnummer?
FRAU PAESCH	Siebenunddreißig . . .
HR. PERLBACH	Siebenunddreißig . . .
FRAU PAESCH	Vierzig . . .
HR. PERLBACH	Vierzig . . .
FRAU PAESCH	Sechsundzwanzig . . .
HR. PERLBACH	Sechsundzwanzig. Danke schön.

This is Siemens, London. Is Herr Paulig in the office?

FRAU PIELKE	*(answering the phone)* Siemens AG, Sekretariat Herr Mehloch. Guten Tag.
FRAU BLUM	Hier Siemens London, Frau Blum. Guten Tag. Ist Herr Paulig im Büro?
FRAU PIELKE	Der Herr Paulig ist da. Darf ich Sie

	verbinden, Frau Blum?
FRAU BLUM	Ja, bitte.
FRAU PIELKE	Kleinen Moment, ich stell' Sie durch.
FRAU BLUM	Danke.
FRAU PIELKE	Auf Wiederhören.
FRAU BLUM	Wiederhören.

I'd like to speak to Herr Gehrels. When's the meeting over? Right, I'll call again then.

FRAU VERTIC	Siemens AG, das Büro von Herrn Gehrels. Guten Morgen.
FRAU BLUM	Guten Tag. Siemens London, Frau Blum hier. Ich möchte gerne Herrn Gehrels sprechen.
FRAU VERTIC	Oh, das tut mir leid. Herr Gehrels ist in einer Besprechung.
FRAU BLUM	Wann ist denn die Besprechung zu Ende?
FRAU VERTIC	So gegen zehn Uhr.
FRAU BLUM	Ja, gut, dann ruf' ich gegen zehn Uhr wieder an.

SOCIALIZING

Are you married? Yes, I have two sons and a small daughter.

FRAU PAGITZ	Herr Göttsch, sind Sie verheiratet?
DR. GÖTTSCH	Ja.
FRAU PAGITZ	Und haben Sie Kinder?
DR. GÖTTSCH	Ja, ich habe zwei Söhne und eine kleine Tochter.
FRAU PAGITZ	Und wie heißen sie?
DR. GÖTTSCH	Meine Söhne heißen Peter und Klaus, und das Mädchen heißt Karin.
FRAU PAGITZ	Und wie alt sind die Kinder?
DR. GÖTTSCH	Peter ist fünfzehn, Klaus ist acht, und Karin ist gerade drei Monate alt.

WORD LIST

der Ingenieur	engineer (with university degree)
die Firma	company
GmbH (Gesellschaft mit beschränkter Haftung)	Ltd
waschen und föhnen	wash and blow dry
machen wir das	let's do that
ich trag' Sie ein	I'll put you down
bis dann	till then
ich muß nachsehen	I must have a look
erstmal	first
bei Ihnen	for/with you
es ginge	it would be possible
der Pförtner	porter, doorman
ich melde Sie an	I'll tell them you're here
die ist . . .	it is . . .
zwo = zwei	two
verbinden	to connect
ich stell' Sie durch	I'll put you through
AG (Aktiengesellschaft)	joint stock company
die Besprechung	meeting
das Mädchen	girl
gerade	just
drei Monate	three months

EXPLANATIONS

WHAT'S YOUR JOB?

In English you say, 'I'm an engineer, I'm a representative', but in German you don't need a word for 'a' or 'an'. You just say: *ich bin Ingenieur, ich bin Vertreter*

Many (though not all) female occupations end with -in:

	MASCULINE	FEMININE
doctor	*Arzt*	*Ärztin*
export manager	*Exportleiter*	*Exportleiterin*
teacher	*Lehrer*	*Lehrerin*
taxi driver	*Taxifahrer*	*Taxifahrerin*
salesclerk	*Verkäufer*	*Verkäuferin*
representative	*Vertreter*	*Vertreterin*

WHERE DO YOU WORK?

To say where you work use *bei*; to say which company you're from use *von*:

ich arbeite bei (der Firma) Neuberger Meßinstrumente
ich bin von (der) Firma Polyband

Although it's *die Firma*, after *bei* und *von*, *die* changes to *der*. In the same way *der* and *das* change to *dem*. The same happens after *aus*, *mit*, *nach* and *zu*:

kommt etwas aus der Minibar dazu?
fahren Sie mit dem Auto?
wie komme ich zur (= zu der) Ost-West-Straße?
nach dem Frühstück machen wir eine Stadtrundfahrt

TIMES OF DAY

yesterday	*gestern*	morning	*der Vormittag*
today	*heute*	afternoon	*der Nachmittag*
tomorrow	*morgen*	evening	*der Abend*

So:

10 a.m.	*zehn Uhr vormittags*
10 p.m.	*zehn Uhr abends*
yesterday afternoon	*gestern nachmittag*
this evening	*heute abend*

tomorrow morning   *morgen vormittag* (or, like Frau
                  Harrington, you can say: *morgen früh*)

ICH MÖCHTE GERNE . . . SPRECHEN

A small group of verbs (called modal verbs) are not complete
on their own. They almost always need another verb to
complete them:
ich **möchte** *gerne Herrn Gehrels* **sprechen**
darf *ich Sie* **verbinden**?
da **muß** *ich erst* **nachsehen.**
kann *ich Ihnen* **helfen**?

WIE HEISSEN SIE?

Sie (with a capital letter) means 'you', but *sie* (with a small
letter) means 'they'. So Frau Pagitz' question asking the
names of Dr. Göttsch's children is written: *wie heißen sie?*
With a small letter, *sie* can also mean 'she' or, if you are
referring to a feminine noun, 'it'. The word for 'he', or 'it' if
you're referring to a masculine noun, is *er*.

ABOUT VERBS

When you look up a verb in a dictionary, you usually find the
'infinitive', e.g. *gehen* to go, *kommen* to come, *heißen* to be
called. From this you can work out the various parts of the
verb. With *ich* the ending is usually *-e*, with *er* (he/it), *sie* (she/
it) and *es* (it) it's usually *-t* and with *wir* (we), *Sie* (you) and *sie*
(they), *-en*:

	gehen	*kommen*	*heißen*
	(to go)	(to come)	(to be called)
ich	*gehe*	*komme*	*heiße*
er, sie, es	*geht*	*kommt*	*heißt*
wir, Sie, sie	*gehen*	*kommen*	*heißen*

There are, of course, exceptions. Among them the two most common verbs of all:

	sein	*haben*
	(to be)	(to have)
ich	*bin*	*habe*
er, sie, es	*ist*	*hat*
wir, Sie, sie	*sind*	*haben*

EXERCISES

APPOINTMENTS

1 These diary entries might have been made by the people in the recordings. Fill them in on the diary page and add the times. Today is Tuesday. Times in German are written like this: 8 o'clock – *8h*; 11:30 – *11.30h*.

T E R M I N E I N D I E S E R W O C H E	
MONTAG	
DIENSTAG	
MITTWOCH	
DONNERSTAG	
PREITAG	
SONNABEND	
SONNTAG	

HERR BERGHEIM	Produktmeeting, Herr Dünker
HERR VON STETTEN	Audi, Herr Seel
SIE (see Exercise 4)	Mercedes, Herr Tasche

DIRECTORY ASSISTANCE

2 You want to make a call to Mercedes-Benz. You ring directory assistance, *die Auskunft, (elf achtundachtzig)* to ask for the number.

AUSKUNFT	*(answering the phone)* Auskunft, Platz dreizehn.★ Guten Tag.
SIE	(Hello, you'd like the number of Mercedes-Benz in Stuttgart.)
AUSKUNFT	Einen Moment bitte. Ja, hier hab' ich sie: siebenundvierzig, dreiundfünfzig, null.
SIE	(And what's the code for Stuttgart?)
AUSKUNFT	Die Vorwahl ist null, sieben, elf.
SIE	(Thank you and goodbye.)
AUSKUNFT	Wiederhör'n.

★Directory assistance gives the seat number, so that you can trace who you've spoken to.

GETTING THROUGH

3 You ring Mercedes-Benz.

FRAU SCHMIDT	*(answering the phone)* Mercedes-Benz, Stuttgart. Schmidt, guten Tag.
SIE	(Greet her and say you'd like to speak to the personnel manager, *den Personalchef*.)
FRAU SCHMIDT	Es tut mir leid, aber Herr Tasche ist in einer Konferenz. Kann ich ihm etwas ausrichten, *give him a message?*
SIE	(No, thanks. Ask when the meeting will be over.)
FRAU SCHMIDT	Ich denke, so gegen vierzehn Uhr.
SIE	(Fine, you'll call again at about 2 o'clock.)
FRAU SCHMIDT	Gut. Herr Tasche hat eine Durchwahl-nummer: siebenundvierzig, dreiundfünfzig, achtunddreißig, zwölf.
SIE	(Repeat the number in English as you write it down. Then say thank you and goodbye.)
FRAU SCHMIDT	Danke für Ihren Anruf. Auf Wiederhören.

FIXING A TIME

4 At 2 o'clock you phone again and get through.

SIE	(Tell Herr Tasche you'd like to visit, *besuchen,* him. And ask if it's possible on Friday afternoon.)
HERR TASCHE	Einen Moment, bitte. Da muß ich erst im Terminkalender nachsehen . . . Tja, Freitag ist schlecht, aber Sonnabend vormittag ginge es.
SIE	(Ask if it would be possible at 10:30.)
HERR TASCHE	Ja gut, um halb elf ist in Ordnung.

ARRIVING FOR AN APPOINTMENT

5 You arrive on Saturday at 10:30. Greet the doorman and say you have an appointment. Tell him what time it is and who it's with.

PFÖRTNER	Guten Morgen. Kann ich Ihnen helfen?
SIE	_____ .
PFÖRTNER	Augenblick bitte, ich melde Sie eben an.
SIE	(Thank him.)

PERSONAL DETAILS

6 Over a cup of coffee after the meeting you have a chat. You're married with one son James, who's 16 years old. What do you tell Herr Tasche?

HERR TASCHE	Sagen Sie, sind Sie verheiratet?
SIE	_____ .
HERR TASCHE	Und haben Sie Kinder?
SIE	_____ .
HERR TASCHE	Wie heißt er denn?
SIE	_____ .
HERR TASCHE	Und wie alt ist James?
SIE	_____ .

HERR TASCHE	Ich würde Sie gern mal besuchen. Ich bin nächste Woche in London. Sagen Sie, wie ist Ihre Telefonnummer?
SIE	(3 57 65 19. Try it in pairs!)
HERR TASCHE	Und die Vorwahl?
SIE	(071)
HERR TASCHE	Gut, dann ruf' ich Sie an, wenn ich in London bin. Bis dann!

DIRECTORY ASSISTANCE AGAIN

7 You have to phone computer companies in different German cities to obtain quotations. You phone directory assistance again and get the following information. Fill it in on the address page below.

ANSCHRIFTEN		
FIRMA	**ORT**	**TELEFON**

IBM, Stuttgart
null einhundertdreißig*/fünfundvierzig, siebenundsechzig

Panasonic, Hamburg
null vierzig/fünfundachtzig, neunundvierzig, siebenundzwanzig, sechsundsiebzig

Tandon Computer GmbH, Frankfurt/Main
null neunundsechzig/vier, zwanzig, fünfundneunzig, einhundertdreiundachtzig

Laser Computer GmbH, Düsseldorf
null, zwo, elf/neunundfünfzig, achtundvierzig,
dreiundneunzig

NEC Deutschland GmbH, München
null, neunundachtzig/neun, dreißig, null, sechs, null

Epson Deutschland GmbH, Düsseldorf
null, zwo, elf/sechsundfünfzig, null, drei, null

Plantron Computer GmbH, Bad Homburg
null, einundsechzig, zweiundsiebzig/fünfundzwanzig,
einhundertachtundachtzig

*null einhundertdreißig is a toll-free number like 800 in the United States.

WORTH KNOWING

ENGINEERS AND TECHNICIANS

In Germany an *Ingenieur* has studied at a university
(*Diplomingenieur*) or at a technical college (*graduierter
Ingenieur*). All other engineers are called *Techniker*
(technicians).

TELEPHONE NUMBERS

Like Frau Paesch, people often give their telephone numbers
in pairs:
siebenunddreißig, vierzig, sechsundzwanzig
This is also the way they're listed in the telephone directory:
37 40 26
If an odd figure is left over, it looks and sounds like this:
7 84 67, *sieben, vierundachtzig, siebenundsechzig.*
If the number is short, it can be grouped in hundreds: 0 130/
324 would be *null, einhundertdreißig/dreihundertvierundzwanzig.*

People often say *zwo* instead of *zwei:*

zwei	*zwo*
zweiundzwanzig	*zwoundzwanzig*
einhundertzwei	*einhundertzwo*

This is to avoid any confusion with *drei.*

TELEPHONING

Phone booths throughout Germany are yellow, but will change to white in the near future. You need at least 30 pfennigs to make a call, or you can buy a phone card (12 DM for 40 units) from the post office. You can make international calls from most phone booths.

Of course, you can call from your hotel as well, but it's likely to be expensive. A unit often costs twice as much as from a booth or from the post office. As yet very few phone booths can receive calls: a bell sign on the door indicates where they do.

Normal rates apply Mondays to Fridays from 8 a.m. to 6 p.m. At all other times telephoning, even internationally, is considerably cheaper.

German telephone signals are different from those in the UK and USA. When you lift the receiver you'll hear a continuous beeping sound. After dialing, the same sound with interruptions indicates that you're through. If you hear short *tüt-tüt-tüt* sounds, you'll know the line is engaged.

SENDING A FAX

If you want to use a fax machine, see if there's one in your hotel. From there it will be much cheaper than from the post office. The hotel will charge you by the unit, while at the post office you pay a very high fixed rate for each page.

CAN YOU *GET BY* ?

Try this section when you've finished the course. If you get it all right you should be able to *Get by!*

MEETING PEOPLE

1 You arrive in Hamburg at 9:30 a.m. and a friend has come to meet you. How do you greet him?
a Guten Morgen
b Guten Tag
c Guten Abend
d Auf Wiedersehen

2 You haven't met his wife, so you introduce yourself to her: _____ .

3 Then you ask her what her name is: _____ ?

4 She asks you: *Wie geht es Ihnen?*
What do you say after enjoying a smooth flight from London to Hamburg? _____ .

5 She asks you: *Woher kommen Sie?*
She wants to know:
a where you're going
b where you're from

c where you're staying
d when you're leaving
e how long you're staying

6 You all go into a bar for a drink. You order. Your friend wants a pot of coffee, his wife would like a coke, and you want to try the famous German beer. What do you say to the waiter? _____ .

7 When you order the beer the waiter asks you: *Ein großes oder ein kleines?*
Does that mean:
a a warm or cold one?
b a large or small one?
c a light or dark one?
d an ale or a lager?

SHOPPING

8 Next morning you go out to do some shopping. At the supermarket you want 100g of Dutch cheese. What do you say?
a Ein Pfund Holländer,
b Zweihundert Gramm Holländer,
c Hundert Gramm Schweizer,
d Hundert Gramm Holländer,
e Zweihundert Gramm Engländer,

bitte.

9 At a market stand you decide to buy a kilo of tomatoes and three bananas. What do you say? _____ .

10 At the post office you ask how much the postage is for a postcard to the United States. Then you buy three stamps:

SIE	_____.
BEAMTER	Eine Postkarte nach Großbritannien kostet sechzig Pfennig.
SIE	_____.

11 At the bank you want to cash a check. You need 350,– DM. You have to write the sum in words:

_____ Deutsche Mark

12 The bank clerk tells you: *Bitte unterschreiben Sie hier.*
Does he want you to:
a write in the amount of money you want?
b write in the date?
c write in your name in block letters?
d sign your name here?
e write in your address?

FINDING SOMEWHERE TO STAY

13 A few days later you travel south to Munich. You've reserved a room in advance at the Münchener Hof. When you arrive there, what do you say?
a Ich möchte ein Zimmer reservieren.
b Haben Sie ein Zimmer frei?
c Ich habe ein Zimmer reserviert.

14 The girl at the reception desk can't remember what kind of room you've reserved. You want a single room with bath. What do you say?
a Ein Doppelzimmer mit Bad, bitte.
b Ein Einzelzimmer mit Dusche, bitte.
c Ein Einzelzimmer mit Bad, bitte.
d Ein Doppelzimmer mit Dusche, bitte.

15 The receptionist tells you: *Mit Frühstück macht das fünfundachtzig Mark pro Nacht.*
The room costs:
a 85,– DM with breakfast
b 58,– DM with breakfast
c 85,– DM without breakfast
d 58,– DM without breakfast

16 You need a taxi and phone the reception desk to ask for one. Your room number is 97.

SIE _____ .

EMPFANG   Ja, sicher. Wie ist, bitte, Ihre Zimmernummer?

SIE _____ .

GETTING ABOUT

17 The taxi takes you right into the city. As you need some medicine, you ask the taxi driver where you can find a pharmacy. What do you say?
Wo gibt es hier . . .
a eine Bank?
b ein Postamt?
c eine Apotheke?
d eine Bushaltestelle?
e eine Kunsthalle?

18 The pharmacy is in the pedestrian zone, so the driver drops you off and gives you directions:
Sie gehen hier geradeaus, dann rechts und dann gleich die zweite Straße links. Sie ist dann auf der linken Seite.
Where do you go?
a right/next right/third left/it's on the right
b straight ahead/right/second left/it's on the left
c straight ahead/left/second right/it's on the right
d left/right/first left/it's on the left

19 Next you want to visit Munich's famous art museum, *die Pinakothek*. You ask a passer-by the best way to get there:

_____ ?

20 You want to know how long it will take you on foot:

_____ ?

21 It would take half an hour so you decide to go by bus. You ask how long that would take: _____ ?

22 Next, you ask where the nearest bus stop is:

_____ ?

23 You are told: *Die Haltestelle ist gleich hier um die Ecke.*
Is the bus stop:
a right in front of you?
b right behind you?
c straight ahead?
d just around the corner?
e a long way from here?

EATING OUT

24 After your visit to the art museum you feel really hungry and go into a restaurant for a meal. You call the waiter and ask for the menu: _____ .

Before the meal you drink a sherry (**25**). You want to have soup (**26**) as an appetizer, a good helping of meat (**27**) for the main course, and ice cream (**28**) for dessert. You'd like to drink red wine (**29**) with your meal and a cup of coffee (**30**) afterward. Under which sections of the menu would you find them?

a Vorspeisen
b Suppen
c Fleischgerichte
d Fischspezialitäten
e Nachspeisen
f Eiskarte
g Biere
h Weine
i Aperitifs und Schnäpse
j alkoholfreie Getränke
k heiße Getränke

31 As you have problems in understanding the menu, you ask the waiter what he'd recommend: _____ ?

32 You don't know what that is either, so you ask:

_____ ?

33 You decide to follow the waiter's recommendation and have the dish. What do you say? _____ .

34 When the waiter serves the meal he says: *Guten Appetit!* That means:
a enjoy your meal
b anything else?
c please pay now
d please hurry up

35 After the meal you ask for the check. What do you say?

_____ .

36 The waiter tells you: *Das macht sechsundfünfzig Mark fünfzig.* What's that in figures? _____ DM

37 You pay with a hundred mark note. What does the waiter say as he gives you your change?
Bitte sehr . . .
a   vierunddreißig Mark fünfzig zurück
b   einundvierzig Mark fünfzig zurück
c   zweiundfünfzig Mark fünfzig zurück
d   dreiundvierzig Mark fünfzig zurück

38 Do you remember the German currency denominations?
What are the fewest notes and coins you can expect as change?

_____ .

39 After you've received your change you give the waiter a tip. What do you say?
a   stimmt so!
b   das ist für Sie!

DOWN TO BUSINESS

40 Next day you phone the computer company NEC in Munich to arrange an appointment with the sales manager (*der Verkaufsleiter*). What do you say?
a   Wie ist Ihre Telefonnummer bei der Firma NEC?
b   Ich habe einen Termin beim Verkaufsleiter.
c   Ich möchte, bitte, den Verkaufsleiter sprechen.

41 He's not there but his secretary gives you the number of his direct line: *neunhundertdreißig, null, sechs, vierhundertfünf.*
You write it down in figures: _____ .

42 She also asks you: *Ginge es heute vormittag?*
What does she want to know?
Would it be all right . . .

a this afternoon?
b tomorrow morning?
c this morning?
d tomorrow afternoon?
e this lunchtime?

43   You make an appointment with Herr Fischer for 11. At the NEC reception you are greeted by the doorman. You introduce yourself, and tell him where you come from (Joy Computers, London), the time of your appointment and who it's with. What do you say? _____ .

44   After the meeting Herr Fischer asks you a few personal questions. You're an import manager (*der Importleiter*) at Joy Computers, and are married with three children, Mary (3), Jane (7) and Gordon (11). What are your answers?

HERR FISCHER   Was sind Sie von Beruf?

SIE   _____ .

HERR FISCHER   Und wo arbeiten Sie?

SIE   _____ .

HERR FISCHER   Sind Sie verheiratet?

SIE   _____ .

HERR FISCHER   Haben Sie auch Kinder?

SIE   _____ .

HERR FISCHER   Und wie heißen sie?

SIE   _____ .

HERR FISCHER   Wie alt sind denn die Kinder?

SIE   _____ .

REFERENCE SECTION

PRONUNCIATION

German pronunciation isn't really difficult. The best way to get it right is to listen carefully to the cassettes and copy what you hear as closely as possible. This pronunciation guide is recorded at the end of the second cassette with pauses for you to repeat the words. Go through it as often as you like until you feel really confident.

VOWELS

Vowels can be long or short. Double vowels are long, as in *Tee, Kaffee*. And vowels are long before an *h*, as in *gehen*. Before a double consonant they're short, as in *Herr, Zimmer*.

a	long	*Sahne, haben*
	or short	*danke, Flasche*
e	long	*gehen, Bremen*
	or short	*gern, Herr*
i	long	*Ihnen, Kilo*
	or short	*bitte, ist*
o	long	*groß, oder*
	or short	*kommen, kostet*
u	long	*gut, Dusche*
	or short	*zum, Pfund*

VOWELS WITH *UMLAUTS*

These have no English equivalents. Listen to the cassette and copy the pronunciation as closely as you can.

ä	long	*Käse, ungefähr*
	or short	*Kännchen, Äpfel*
ö	long	*schön*
	or short	*möchte*
ü	long	*für, Menü*
	or short	*fünf, Stück*

VOWEL COMBINATIONS

au	like 'ow' in 'how'	*Frau, aus*
ai ⎫	like 'y' in 'my'	*Mai*
ei ⎭		*Wein*
ie	like 'ee' in 'tree'	*die, hier*
äu ⎫	like 'oy' in 'toy'	*Fräulein*
eu ⎭		*Deutsch*

CONSONANTS

Most sound similar to English, but there are some points to notice.

ch	after *a, o, u* and *au* like 'ch' in the Scottish 'loch'.	*macht, noch* *Kuchen, auch*
	Otherwise like 'h' in huge	*ich, rechts*
chs	like 'x' in 'sex'	*sechs*
d	at the end of a word like 't'	*Bad*
-ig	at the end of a word, usually as in *ich*	*zwanzig*
j	like 'y' in 'you'	*ja, Jahr*
r	rolled from the back of the throat	*rot, rechts*
sch	like 'sh' in 'shop'	*Schlüssel, Flasche*
sp	at the beginning of a word, 'shp'	*Speisekarte, sprechen*

st	at the beginning of a word, 'sht'	*Stück, Straße*
v	like 'f' in 'for'	*vier, von*
w	like 'v' in 'vine'	*weit, auf Wiedersehen*
z	like 'ts' in 'cats'	*zehn, zu*

NUMBERS

0	*null*	10	*zehn*	20	*zwanzig*
1	*eins*	11	*elf*	21	*einundzwanzig*
2	*zwei*	12	*zwölf*	22	*zweiundzwanzig*
3	*drei*	13	*dreizehn*	23	*dreiundzwanzig*
4	*vier*	14	*vierzehn*	24	*vierundzwanzig*
5	*fünf*	15	*fünfzehn*	25	*fünfundzwanzig*
6	*sechs*	16	*sechzehn*	26	*sechsundzwanzig*
7	*sieben*	17	*siebzehn*	27	*siebenundzwanzig*
8	*acht*	18	*achtzehn*	28	*achtundzwanzig*
9	*neun*	19	*neunzehn*	29	*neunundzwanzig*

30	*dreißig*	80	*achtzig*
40	*vierzig*	90	*neunzig*
50	*fünfzig*	100	*hundert*
60	*sechzig*	200	*zweihundert*
70	*siebzig*	1000	*tausend*

PRICES AND TIMES

These are usually written as follows:

Prices	35 DM	*fünfunddreißig Mark*
	2,58 DM	*zwei Mark achtundfünfzig*
Times	11.16 Uhr	*elf Uhr sechzehn*
	18.38 Uhr	*achtzehn Uhr achtunddreißig*

DAYS OF THE WEEK

Sonntag	Sunday	*Donnerstag*	Thursday
Montag	Monday	*Freitag*	Friday
Dienstag	Tuesday	*Samstag* or	Saturday
Mittwoch	Wednesday	*Sonnabend*	

MONTHS OF THE YEAR

Januar	January	*Juli*	July
Februar	February	*August*	August
März	March	*September*	September
April	April	*Oktober*	October
Mai	May	*November*	November
Juni	June	*Dezember*	December

WEIGHTS AND MEASURES

The metric system is used in German-speaking Europe. The
following will help you convert your customary measurement
units into their metric equivalents.

CENTIMETERS/INCHES

To convert centimeters into inches, multiply by 0.39.
To convert inches into centimeters, multiply by 2.54.

METERS/FEET

1 meter = 39.37 inches	1 foot = 0.3 meters
3.28 feet	1 yard = 0.9 meters
1.09 yards	

KILOGRAMS/POUNDS

1 kilogram (kilo) = 2.2 pounds
1 pound = 0.45 kilograms

LITERS/QUARTS

1 liter = 1.06 quarts
4 liters = 1.06 gallons
For quick, approximate conversions, multiply the number of
gallons by 4 to get liters. Divide the number of liters by 4 to get
gallons.

THE FOUR SEASONS

spring	**der Frühling**	*dehr FREW-ling*
summer	**der Sommer**	*dehr ZOM-uh*
autumn	**der Herbst**	*dehr hehrpst*
winter	**der Winter**	*dehr VINT-uh*
during the spring	**während des**	*VEHR-ent dehs*
	Frühlings	*FREW-lings*
every summer	**jeden Sommer**	*YAYD-en ZOM-uh*
in the winter	**im Winter**	*im VINT-uh*

TEMPERATURE CONVERSIONS

To change Fahrenheit to Centigrade, subtract 32 and multiply by ⅝.

To change Centigrade to Fahrenheit, multiply by ⅝ and add 32.

Grad
Hundertgradig Fahrenheit

Thermometer

ROAD SIGNS

Ausfahrt Frei Halten	Keep Driveway Clear
Blaue Zone	Blue Parking Zone (requires special parking disk)
Durchgangs-Verkehr	Through Traffic
Einbahn-Strasse	One-way Street
Ende des Park-Verbots	End of No Parking Zone
Fussgänger-Zone	Pedestrian Zone
Gefährliches Gefälle	Dangerous Descent
Gefährliche Steigung	Dangerous (steep) Hill
Halt, Polizei	Stop, Police
Kein Durchgang Für Fussgänger	Closed to Pedestrians
Kurzparkzone	Limited Parking Zone
Langsam Fahren	Drive Slowly
Lawinenge fahr	Danger of Avalanche
Links Fahren	Keep Left
Nur Für Anlieger	Residents Only
Parken Verboten	No Parking
Rechts Fahren	Keep Right
Schlechte Fahrbahn	Bad Road Surface
Umleitung	Detour
____ **Verboten**	____ Not Allowed

Danger ahead

Entrance to expressway

Expressway ends

ROAD SIGNS

Border crossing

Guarded railroad crossing

Yield

Stop

Traffic circle (roundabout) ahead

Right of way

Dangerous intersection ahead

Gasoline (petrol) ahead

No passing

Parking

No vehicles allowed

Dangerous curve

No U-turn

Pedestrian crossing

Oncoming traffic has right of way

No bicycles allowed

Traffic signal ahead

No parking allowed

No entry

No left turn

Speed limit

Minimum speed limit

All traffic turns left

End of no passing zone

One-way street

Detour

OTHER IMPORTANT SIGNS

Abfahrten	Departures
Achtung	Attention
Aufzug	Elevator
Ausfahrt	Highway Exit
Ausgang	Exit
Auskunft	Information
Belegt	Filled Up
Besetzt	Occupied
Damentoilette	Ladies' room
Drücken	Push
Einfahrt	Highway Entrance
Eingang	Entrance
Eintritt frei	No Admission Charge
Frei	Vacant
Für Unbefugte verboten	No Trespassing
Gefahr	Danger
Geöffnet von ____ bis ____	Open from ____ to ____
Geschlossen	Closed
Herrentoilette	Men's room
Kasse	Cashier
Kein Zutritt	No entry
Lebensgefahr	Mortal danger
Lift	Elevator
Nicht berühren	Do not touch
Notausgang	Emergency exit
Rauchen verboten	No smoking
Raucher	Smoking compartment
Reserviert	Reserved

____ **verboten**	____ prohibited
Vorsicht	Caution
Vorsicht, Bissiger Hund	Beware of the dog
Ziehen	Pull
Zimmer frei	Room(s) to let

MENU ITEMS

SOUPS AND STEWS

Aalsuppe *AAL-zup-eh*	eel soup
Backerbsensuppe *BAHK-ehrps-en-zup-eh*	broth with croutons
Bauernsuppe *BOW-ern-zup-eh*	cabbage and sausage soup
Bohnensuppe *BOHN-en-zup-eh*	bean soup (usually with bacon)
Erbsensuppe *EHRP-sen-zup-eh*	pea soup
Fischsuppe *FISH-zup-eh*	fish soup
Fritattensuppe *free-DAHT-en-zup-eh*	broth with pancake strips
Frühlingssuppe *FREW-lings-zup-eh*	spring vegetable soup
Grießnockerlsuppe *GREES-nok-ehrl-zup-eh*	semolina-dumpling soup
Gerstenbrühe *GEHRST-en-brew-eh*	barley broth
Gulaschsuppe *GOOL-ahsh-zup-eh*	stewed beef in a spicy soup
Hühnerreissuppe *HEWN-er-reyes-zup-eh*	chicken-rice soup

Hummersuppe
HUM-uh-zup-eh
lobster soup

Kalte Obstsuppe, Kaltschale cold fruit soup, usually
KAHLT-eh OHPST-zup-eh, containing cream, beer,
KAHLT-shahl-eh or wine

Kartoffelsuppe
kahr-TOF-el-zup-eh
potato soup

Kartoffellauchsuppe
kahr-TOF-el-LOWKH-zup-eh
potato-leek soup

Knödelsuppe
KNERD-el-zup-eh
dumpling soup

Königinsuppe
KERN-ig-in-zup-eh
contains beef, sour
cream, and almonds

Kraftbrühe mit Ei
KRAFT-brew-eh mit eye
beef consommé with raw egg

Labskaus *LAAPS-kowss*
heavy stew of chopped,
marinated meat with mashed
potatoes and vegetables

Leberknödelsuppe
LAY-behr-knerd-el-zup-eh
liver dumpling soup

Linsensuppe *LINZ-en-zup-eh* lentil soup

Mehlsuppe Basler Art
MAYL-zup-eh BAAZL-uh aart
cheese soup with flour,
Basel style

Nudelsuppe *NOO-del-zup-eh* noodle soup

Ochsenschwanzsuppe
OK-sen-shvahnts-zup-eh
oxtail soup

Pichelsteiner Eintopf
PIKH-el-shteyen-uh EYEN-topf
meat and vegetable stew

Schildkrötensuppe
SHILT-krert-en-zup-eh
turtle soup

Schweinsragoutsuppe
SHVEYENS-rahgoo-zup-eh
pork-ragout soup

Semmelsuppe *ZEH-mel-zup-eh*	dumpling soup
Serbische Bohnensuppe *ZERB-ish-eh BOHN-en-zup-eh*	spicy bean soup
Spargelsuppe *SHPAHR-gel-zup-eh*	asparagus soup
Tomatensuppe *toh-MAT-en-zup-eh*	tomato soup
Zwiebelsuppe *TSVEE-bel-zup-eh*	onion soup

MEATS

Bauernomelett *BOW-ehrn-om-let*	bacon and onion omelet
Bauernschmaus *BOW-ehrn-shmowss*	sauerkraut with smoked pork, sausages, dumplings, and potatoes
Bauernwurst *BOW-ehrn-voorst*	pork sausage with mustard seeds and peppercorns
Bratwurst *BRAAT-voorst*	fried sausage
Bündnerfleisch (Swiss) *BEWND-nehr-fleyesh*	thinly sliced, air-dried beef
deutsches Beefsteak *DOY-ches BEEF-stayk*	Salisbury steak, hamburger
Eisbein *EYES-beyen*	pig's knuckle
Faschiertes (Aust.) *fah-SHEERT-es*	chopped meat
Fiakergulasch (Aust.) *fee-AHK-un-goo-lahsh*	goulash topped with a fried egg
Frikadellen *fri-kah-DELL-en*	croquettes
gefülltes Kraut *geh-FEWLT-es krowt*	cabbage leaves stuffed with chopped meat, rice, eggs, and bread crumbs

Gehacktes *ge-HAHKT-es* — chopped meat

Geschnetzeltes (Swiss) *ge-SHNEH-tsel-tes* — braised veal tips

Geselchtes *ge-ZEHLKHT-es* — salty smoked meat (pork)

Gulasch *GOO-lahsh* — beef stew with spicy paprika gravy

Hackbraten *HAHK-braat-en* — meatloaf

Hackfleisch *HAHK-fleyesh* — chopped meat

Hammelbraten *HAHM-el-braat-en* — roast mutton

Hammelkeule, Hammelschlegel *HAHM-el-koyl-eh, HAHM-el-shlay-gel* — leg of mutton

Hammelrippchen *HAHM-el-rip-khen* — mutton chops

Herz *hehrts* — heart

Holsteiner Schnitzel *HOL-shteyen-uh SHNITS-el* — breaded veal cutlet topped with a fried egg

Jungfernbraten *YUNG-fehrn-braat-en* — a crunchy roast suckling pig

Kalbsbraten *KAHLPS-braat-en* — roast veal

Kalbsbrust *KAHLPS-brust* — breast of veal

Kalbshachse *KAHLPS-hahks-eh* — veal shank

Kalbsmilch *KAHLPS-milkh* — sweetbreads

Karbonade *kahr-bo-NAAD-eh* — fried rib pork chops

Klöße *KLERSS-eh* — meatballs

Kohl und Pinkel *kohl unt PINK-el*	smoked meat, cabbage, and potatoes
Kohlroulade *KOHL-roo-laad-eh*	stuffed cabbage
Königsberger Klops *KER-niks-behrg-uh Klops*	meatballs in caper sauce
-kotelett *-kot-LET*	chop, cutlet
Kutteln *KUT-ehln*	tripe
Lammkotelett *LAHM-kot-LET*	lamb chop
Leber *LAY-buh*	liver
Leberkäs *LAY-buh-kays*	meatloaf
Lendenbraten *LEHND-en-braat-en*	roast sirloin, tenderloin
Medaillons *mehd-eye-YONGS*	little discs of veal or pork
Naturschnitzel *nah-TOOR-shni-tsel*	thick, unbreaded veal cutlet
Nieren *NEER-en*	kidneys
Pöckelfleisch *PER-kel-fleyesh*	pickled meat
Rinderbraten *RIND-uh-braat-en*	roast beef
Rindsstück *RINTS-shtewk*	steak, slice of beef
Rippensteak *RIP-ehn-shtayk*	rib steak
Rouladen *roo-LAAD-en*	vegetables rolled up in thick slices of beef or veal
Rumpfstück *RUMPF-shtewk*	rump steak
Sauerbraten *ZOW-ehr-braat-en*	marinated pot roast in a spicy brown gravy
Schlachtplatte *SHLAHKHT-plaht-eh*	mixed sausages and cold meats
Schmorfleisch *SHMOHR-fleyesh*	stewed meat

Schnitzel *SHNITS-el*	cutlet (usually veal)
Schweinskotelett *SHVEYENS-kot-let*	pork chop
Spanferkel *SHPAAN-fehr-kel*	suckling pig
Speck *shpehk*	bacon
(Steierische) Brettjause *SHTEYE-uh-rish-eh BREHT-yowz-eh*	(Styrian) cold cuts on a wooden platter
Sülze *Zewlts-eh*	headcheese ("brawn" in Britain)
Tafelspitz *TAAF-el-shpits*	Viennese boiled beef
Tartarensteak *tahr-TAAR-en-shtayk*	ground raw beef, seasoned variously
Wiener Schnitzel *VEEN-uh SHNITS-el*	breaded veal cutlet
Zigeuner Schnitzel *tsee-GOYN-uh SHNITS-el*	veal or pork cutlet in a sharp sauce
Zunge *TSUNG-eh*	tongue

POULTRY AND GAME

Backhuhn *BAHK-hoon*	fried chicken
Brathuhn *BRAAT-hoon*	roast chicken
Entenbraten *EHNT-en-braat-en*	roast duck
Fasan *fah-ZAAN*	pheasant
Gänsebraten *GEHN-zeh-braat-en*	roast goose
Hähnchen *HAYN-khen*	small chicken
Hasenbraten *HAAZ-en-braat-en*	roast hare
Hirschbraten	venison

HEERSH-braat-en

Hühnerbraten roast chicken
HEWN-ehr-braat-en

Kaninchen *kah-NEEN-khen* rabbit

Rebhuhn *RAYP-hoon* partridge

Taube *TOW-beh* pigeon, dove, squab

Truthahn *TROOT-haan* turkey

Wachtel *VAHKHT-el* quail

FISH AND SEAFOOD

Aal *aal* eel

Austern *OW-stern* oysters

Barsch *bahrsh* (lake) perch

Brachse/Brasse bream
BRAHKS-eh/BRAHSS-eh

Dorsch *dorsh* cod

Felchen *FEHL-khen* whiting

Forelle *for-EHL-eh* trout

Flunder *FLUND-uh* flounder

Garnelen *gahr-NAYL-en* shrimp, prawns

Hecht *hekht* pike

Heilbutt *HEYEL-but* halibut

Hering *HAY-ring* herring

Hummer *HUM-uh* lobster

Jakobsmuscheln scallops
YAA-kops-mush-eln

Junger Hecht pickerel
YUNG-uh hekht

Kabeljau *KAA-bel-yow* cod

Karpfen *KAHR-pfen* carp

Krabben *KRAH-ben*	shrimp, prawn
Krebs *krayps*	crab
Lachs *lahks*	salmon
Languste *lahn-GOOST-eh*	lobster
Makrele *mah-KRAY-leh*	mackerel
Muscheln *MUSH-eln*	clams, mussels
Rogen *ROH-gen*	roe
Schellfisch *SHEHL-fish*	haddock
Scholle *SHOL-eh*	flatfish, plaice
Schwertfisch *SHVAYRT-fish*	swordfish
Seebarsch *ZAY-bahrsh*	sea bass
Seezunge *ZAY-tsung-eh*	sole
Steinbutt *SHTEYEN-but*	turbot
Stint *shtint*	smelt
Stör *shterr*	sturgeon
Tintenfisch *TINT-en-fish*	squid, cuttlefish
Zander *TSAHND-uh*	pike-perch

VEGETABLES

Auberginen *oh-behr-ZHEEN-en*	eggplant
Blumenkohl *BLOOM-en-kohl*	cauliflower
Bohnen *BOHN-en*	beans
Braunkohl *BROWN-kohl*	kale
Erbsen *EHRPS-en*	peas
Essiggurken *EHSS-ikh-goork-en*	sour pickles (gherkins)
Fisolen (Aust.) *fee-SOHL-en*	string beans, French beans
Gelbe Wurzeln *GEHLB-eh VOORTS-eln*	carrots

Gemischtes Gemüse *geh-MISHT-ehs ge-MEWZ-eh*	mixed vegetables
Grüne Bohnen *GREWN-eh BOHN-en*	green beans
Gurken *GOORK-en*	cucumbers
Kabis, Kappes *KAHB-is, KAHP-es*	cabbage
Karfiol (Aust.) *kahr-fee-OHL*	cauliflower
Karotten *kahr-OT-en*	carrots
Kohl *kohl*	cabbage
Kukuruz (Aust.) *KOOK-oor-oots*	corn, maize
Lauch *lowkh*	leeks
Leipziger Allerlei *LEYEPTS-eeg-uh AHL-uh-leye*	carrots, peas, and asparagus
Mais *meyess*	corn, maise
Paradeiser *pah-rah-DEYEZ-uh*	tomatoes
Pilze *PILTS-eh*	mushrooms
Radieschen *rah-DEES-khen*	radishes
Rosenkohl *ROHZ-en-kohl*	brussels sprouts
Rote Beten (Rüben) *ROHT-eh-BAYT-en (REWB-en)*	beets
Rotkohl (Rotkraut) *ROHT-kohl (ROHT-krowt)*	red cabbage
Rübenkraut *REWB-en-krowt*	turnip tops
Spargelspitzen *SHPAARG-el-shpits-en*	asparagus tips
Spinat *shpeen-AAT*	spinach
Tomaten *to-MAAT-en*	tomatoes
Weiße Bohnen *VEYESS-eh BOHN-en*	white beans

Weiße Rüben turnips
VEYESS-eh REWB-en

Weißkohl *VEYESS-kohl* cabbage

Zwiebeln *TSVEEB-eln* onions

POTATOES AND NOODLES

Bratkartoffeln fried potatoes
BRAAT-kahr-tof-eln

Geröstel *ge-RERST-el* hashed-brown potatoes

Dampfnudeln steamed noodles, vermicelli
DAHMPF-nood-eln

Fadennudeln vermicelli
FAAD-en-nood-eln

Kartoffel(n) *kahr-TOF-el(n)* potato(es)

Krautkrapfen cabbage fritters
KROWT-krahp-fen

Pellkartoffeln unpeeled boiled potatoes
PEHL-kahr-tof-eln

Petersilienkartoffeln parsleyed potatoes
pay-tehr-ZEEL-yen-kahr-toff-eln

Pommes frites *pom frit* french fries

Röstkartoffeln fried potatoes
REWST-kahr-tof-eln

Rösti (Swiss) *REWST-ee* hashed-brown potatoes

Salzkartoffeln boiled potatoes
ZAHLTS-kahr-tof-eln

Spätzle *SHPEHTS-leh* thick noodles or Swabian
dumplings

Teigwaren *TEYEKH-vaar-en* pasta products, noodles

FRUITS

Ananas *AHN-ah-nahss*	pineapple
Apfel *AHPF-el*	apple
Apfelsine *ahpf-el-ZEEN-eh*	orange
Banane *bah-NAAN-eh*	banana
Birne *BEERN-eh*	pear
Blaubeeren *BLOW-bayr-en*	blueberries
Brombeeren *BROM-bayr-en*	blackberries
Erdbeeren *AYRT-bayr-en*	strawberries
Feigen *FEYEG-en*	figs
Granatapfel *grah-NAAT-ahpf-el*	pomegranate
Heidelbeeren *HEYED-el-bayr-en*	blueberries
Himbeeren *HIM-bayr-en*	raspberries
Holunderbeeren *hol-UND-uh-bayr-en*	elderberries
Johannisbeeren *yoh-HAHN-is-bayr-en*	currants
Kirschen *KEERSH-en*	cherries
Mandarine *mahn-dah-REEN-eh*	tangerine
Marillen (Aust.) *mah-RIL-en*	apricots
Melone *meh-LOHN-en*	cantaloupe
Pampelmuse *PAHMP-el-mooz-eh*	grapefruit
Pfirsich *PFEER-zikh*	peach
Pflaumen *PFLOW-men*	plums
Preiselbeeren *PREYE-zel-bayr-en*	cranberries
Quitte *KVIY-eh*	quince

Rauschbeeren   cranberries
ROWSH-bayr-en

Rhabarber *rah-BAHRB-uh*   rhubarb

Rosinen *roh-ZEEN-en*   raisins

Stachelbeeren   gooseberries
SHTAH-khel-bayr-en

Trauben *TROWB-en*   grapes

Wassermelone   watermelon
VAHSS-uh-meh-lohn-eh

Weintrauben   grapes
VEYEN-trowb-en

Zuckermelone   honeydew melon
TSUK-uh-meh-lohn-eh

KEY TO EXERCISES

1 MEETING PEOPLE

HELLO AND GOODBYE

1a Guten Tag! **b** Guten Abend! **c** Hallo, Dieter.
d Tschüs, Dieter.

HOW ARE YOU?

2 Hallo (*or* Guten Tag), Herr Meier./Danke, gut./(wie geht es) Ihnen?/ Danke/gut.

WHERE ARE YOU FROM?

3 Nein, ich bin Schotte *or* Schottin./Aus Edinburgh? Nein, ich bin nicht aus Edinburgh!/Ich komme aus Glasgow.

ORDERING DRINKS

4 Herr Ober!/Ein Bier, bitte./Ein kleines, bitte./Einen Whisky./Mit Eis, bitte.

MORE DRINKS

5 Möchten Sie Kaffee?/Mit Zitrone oder Milch?/Nein, ich möchte Kaffee./Möchten Sie Tee?/Möchten Sie heiße Schokolade?/Eine große oder eine kleine Tasse?/Herr Ober!/ Ein Kännchen Tee, ein Kännchen Kaffee und eine große Tasse heiße Schokolade, bitte.

2 SHOPPING

YOUR SHOPPING LIST

1 Zwei Postkarten, bitte. Fünfhundert Gramm (*or* ein Pfund) Edamer, bitte. Acht Brötchen, bitte. Ein Paket Kekse, bitte. Fünf Rosen, bitte. Eine Flasche Rotwein, bitte. Ein Pfund Äpfel, bitte. Eine Tüte Milch, bitte. **2** 2,37 DM, 24,11 DM, 17,43 DM.

AT THE DELICATESSEN

3 Ich hätte gern (*or* ich möchte gern) dreihundert Gramm Holländer (*or* Dreihundert Gramm Holländer, bitte)./ Geschnitten, bitte./Vielen Dank (*or* Danke schön).

THE FRUIT STAND

4 Ein Kilo Tomaten, bitte./Ja, ein Pfund (*or* fünfhundert Gramm) Bananen, bitte./Haben Sie Kiwis?/Acht Stück, bitte. **5** 10,14 DM (zehn Mark und vierzehn).

AT THE POST OFFICE

6 Wieviel kostet ein Brief nach England?/Ich möchte drei Briefmarken, bitte./Haben Sie Postkarten?/Vier. Wieviel kostet eine (Postkarte)?/ Was macht das, bitte?/Bitte sehr (*or* Bitte schön)./Vielen Dank. Auf Wiedersehen. **7** Two 2 DM notes; two 2 DM coins; one 50 pfennig coin; and one 10 pfennig coin.

CASHING A TRAVELER'S CHECK

8 Guten Tag. Ich möchte gern einen Reisescheck einlösen./ Hier?/Vielen Dank (*or* Danke schön). Auf Wiedersehen. **9** 396,50 DM **10** 3,50 DM.

3 FINDING SOMEWHERE TO STAY

TELEPHONING A HOTEL

1 Guten Tag. Ich hätte gern *or* ich möchte ein Einzelzimmer mit Dusche./Was (*or* wieviel) kostet das (Zimmer)?/Ach, nein danke (*or* Ach, das geht nicht). Auf Wiederhören.

AT THE TOURIST INFORMATION CENTER

2 Ich möchte ein Zimmer reservieren./Ich hätte gern (*or* ich möchte) ein Einzelzimmer mit Dusche./(Für) vier Nächte, bitte./Was (*or* wieviel) kostet das (Zimmer)?/Ja, das nehme ich (*or* Ja, das geht).

CHECKING IN

3 Guten Tag. Mein Name ist . . . Ich habe ein Zimmer reserviert./Mit Dusche./Bitte schön./Können Sie mir ein Taxi bestellen?/Vielen Dank (*or* Danke schön).

ROOM SERVICE

4 Ich hätte gern (*or* ich möchte) eine Flasche Wein./Weißen, bitte./Ja, eine Flasche (Mineral) Wasser, bitte./Danke. Auf Wiederhören.

AT THE CAMPGROUND

5 Haben Sie noch Zeltplätze frei?/Wir sind drei Erwachsene und ein Kind./Ja, ein Auto. Was (*or* wieviel) kosted das?/Ja, das geht.

4 GETTING ABOUT

GOING BY SUBWAY

1 (Entschuldigen Sie bitte,) wo ist die nächste U-Bahn Station? **2** (Entschuldigen Sie bitte,) welche Nummer fährt in die Innenstadt?

FINDING A CAFÉ

3 Entschuldigen Sie bitte, gibt es hier in der Nähe ein Café?/
Ist es weit (von hier)?

WHEN IS THE BANK OPEN?

5 Wann sind Ihre Öffnungszeiten?/Haben Sie samstags (*or*
sonnabends) geöffnet?

6

DEUTSCHE BANK, HAMBURG	
ÖFFNUNGSZEITEN:	
Mo./Di./Mi.:	9.00 Uhr bis 16.30 Uhr
Donnerstag:	9.00 Uhr bis 18.00 Uhr
Freitag:	9.00 Uhr bis 14.30 Uhr
Samstag:	geschlossen

7 Kleine Stadtrundfahrt mit Alster-Bootsfahrt.

5 EATING OUT

SORTING OUT THE MENU

1 c **2** d **3** f **4** e **5** b **6** a

ORDERING A MEAL

7 Ich hätte gern (*or* ich möchte bitte) die Hamburger
Fischsuppe mit Knoblauchbrot. (*or* Die Hamburger
Fischsuppe mit Knoblauchbrot, bitte.)/Als Hauptgang nehme
ich die Nordseescholle mit Büsumer Krabben und
Petersilienkartoffeln./Ich möchte (*or* ich hätte gern) einen
Rheinwein, bitte./Ja, heiße Himbeeren mit Vanille-Eis und
Sahne, bitte.

Menu

Menu

COLD AND WARM APPETIZERS
Salad – fresh from the field
Trout fillet with horseradish sauce, toast and butter
Prawn cocktail

SOUPS
Soup of the day   *Hamburg prawn soup*
Hungarian goulash soup   *Hamburg fish soup with garlic bread*

FISH
Plaice fillet with mushrooms, artichokes and butter potatoes
North Sea plaice with Büsum prawns and parsley potatoes
Salmon steak (grilled) with tomatoes, mushrooms and dill potatoes
Sole fillet with melted butter, boiled potatoes and mixed salad

MEAT
Hamburg Labskaus, tasty side dish
Lamb fillets in garlic sauce, spinach and butter potatoes
Captain's Plate with three small steaks, fresh vegetables and butter potatoes
Pepper steak with parsley potatoes and seasonal salad

DESSERTS
Assorted ice cream with cream   *Ice-coffee with cream*
Hot raspberries with vanilla ice cream and cream

WINE (BY THE GLASS)
Rhine   *Red wine*
Moselle *Franconian* *Rosé*

All prices include service and VAT!

PAYING BY CREDIT CARD

8 Ja, danke. Ausgezeichnet. Bitte, die Rechnung./Ich möchte mit Kreditkarte bezahlen./Ja, sicher. Und das ist für Sie./Auf Wiedersehen.

9
Hamburger Fischsuppe mit Knoblauchbrot:	9,00 DM
Nordseescholle mit Büsumer Krabben und Petersilienkartoffeln:	26,50 DM
Heiße Himbeeren mit Vanille-Eis und Sahne:	9,50 DM
Rheinwein:	7,50 DM
SUMME:	52,50 DM

COFFEE AND CAKE

10 Kaffee und ein Stück Zitronentorte, bitte./Eine Tasse, bitte./Mit Sahne (, bitte).

6 DOWN TO BUSINESS

APPOINTMENTS

1

TERMINE IN DIESER WOCHE	
MONTAG	
DIENSTAG	14h Audi, Herr Seel
MITTWOCH	11h Friseur
DONNERSTAG	
FREITAG	9h Produktmeeting, Herr Dünker
SONNABEND	10.30h Mercedes, Herr Tasche
SONNTAG	

DIRECTORY ASSISTANCE

2 Guten Tag. Ich hätte gern (*or* ich möchte gern) die
Nummer von Mercedes-Benz in Stuttgart./Und wie ist die
Vorwahl von Stuttgart?/Vielen Dank (*or* Danke schön). Auf
Wiederhören.

GETTING THROUGH

3 Guten Tag. Ich möchte gerne den Personalchef sprechen./
Nein, danke. Wann ist die Konferenz zu Ende?/Gut. Ich rufe
gegen vierzehn Uhr wieder an./47 53 38 12. Vielen Dank. Auf
Wiederhören.

FIXING A TIME

4 Guten Tag, Herr Tasche. Ich möchte Sie gern besuchen.
Geht es am Freitag nachmittag?/Ginge es um halb elf (*or* um
zehn Uhr dreißig)?

ARRIVING FOR AN APPOINTMENT

5 Guten Morgen. Ich habe um halb elf einen Termin bei
Herrn Tasche./Vielen Dank (*or* Danke schön).

PERSONAL DETAILS

6 Ja, ich bin verheiratet./Ja, (ich habe) einen Sohn./Er heißt
James./Er ist sechzehn./Drei, siebenundfünfzig,
fünfundsechzig, neunzehn./Null, einundsiebzig.

7 ANSCHRIFTEN

FIRMA	ORT	TELEFON
IBM	Stuttgart	0130-4567
Panasonic	Hamburg	040-854927
Tandon Computer GmbH	Frankfurt/Main	069-420 95183
Laser Computer GmbH	Düsseldorf	0211-594893
NEC Deutschland GmbH	München	089-930060
Epson Deutschland GmbH	Düsseldorf	0211-56030
Plantron Computer GmbH	Bad Homburg	06172-25188

CAN YOU *GET BY*?

MEETING PEOPLE

1 a   **2**   Ich heiße . . . (*or* Mein Name ist . . .)   **3**   Wie
heißen Sie, bitte? (*or* Wie ist Ihr Name, bitte?)   **4**   Danke,
gut.   **5** b   **6**   Ich hätte gern (*or* ich möchte) ein Kännchen
Kaffee, eine Cola und ein Bier (, bitte).   **7** b.

SHOPPING

8 d   **9**   Ich hätte gern (*or* ich möchte) ein Kilo Tomaten und
drei Bananen (, bitte).   **10**   Was (*or* wieviel) kostet eine
Postkarte nach Großbritannien, bitte?/0,60 DM (Ich möchte)
bitte drei Briefmarken   **11**   dreihundertfünfzig   **12** d.

FINDING SOMEWHERE TO STAY

13 c   **14** c   **15** a   **16**   Können Sie mir ein Taxi bestellen? (*or*
Ich hätte gern ein Taxi.)/Siebenundneunzig.

GETTING ABOUT

17 c   **18** b   **19**   Entschuldigen Sie, wie komme ich am besten zur Pinakothek?   **20**   Wie weit ist das zu Fuß?
21   Und (wie weit ist das) mit dem Bus?   **22**   Wo ist die nächste Bushaltestelle?   **23** d.

EATING OUT

24   Herr Ober, die Speisekarte, bitte!   **25** i   **26** b   **27** c
28 f   **29** h   **30** k   **31**   Was würden Sie (denn heute) empfehlen?   **32**   Was ist das, bitte?   **33**   Das nehme ich.   **34** a   **35**   Herr Ober! Die Rechnung, bitte!
36   56,50 DM   **37** d   **38**   two 20 DM notes; one 2 DM coin; one 1 DM coin; one 50 pfennig coin   **39** b.

DOWN TO BUSINESS

40 c   **41**   930 06 405   **42** c   **43**   Mein Name ist . . . Ich komme aus London, (ich bin) von der Firma Joy Computers. Ich habe um elf Uhr einen Termin bei Herrn Fischer.
44   Ich bin Importleiter./Ich arbeite bei (der Firma) Joy Computers in London. Ja./Ich habe zwei Töchter und einen Sohn./Sie heißen Mary, Jane und Gordon./Mary ist drei, Jane ist sieben und Gordon ist elf (Jahre alt).

WORD LIST

Abbreviations: *(m.)* masculine, *(f.)* feminine, *(s.)* singular, *(pl.)* plural, *(refl.)* reflexive verb, *(sep.)* separable verb, *(col.)* colloquial, *(lit.)* literally, *(s. Ger.)* south German. Plural forms of nouns are given in parentheses.

The English meanings apply to the words as they are used in this book.

GERMAN-ENGLISH

A

   à per
die Aalsuppe (-n) eel soup
der Abend (-e) evening;
   guten Abend! good evening!
   das Abendessen (-) dinner
   abends in the evenings
   aber but, also used for emphasis: **das ist aber nett** that's very nice (of you)!
   abfahren *(sep.)* to leave
die Abfahrt (-en) departure
   abholen *(sep.)* to meet, to pick up
   ach oh
die Adresse (-n) address
   AG = Aktiengesellschaft joint stock company
die Allee (-n) avenue
   alles all, everything; **das ist alles** that's all
   als as, for **also** so
   alt old
die Altstadt (¨e) old part of town
   am = an dem at/on the
der Amerikaner American (man)
die Amerikanerin American (woman)

am Donnerstag on Thursday

andere other; **ein anderes Land** another country

die **Ampel (-n)** traffic light

anbieten (*sep.*) to offer

der **Anfang (-̈e)** beginning

der *or* **die Angestellte (-n)** employee, assistant

anmelden to tell someone you're there

der **Anruf (-e)** telephone call

anrufen (*sep.*) to call, to phone

die **Anschrift (-en)** address

die **Antwort (-en)** answer

der **Apfel(-̈)** apple

der **Apfelstrudel (-)** kind of apple pastry

die **Apotheke (-n)** pharmacy

der **Appetit** appetite; **guten Appetit!** enjoy your meal!

die **Arbeit (-en)** work

arbeiten (bei) to work (at)

der **Arzt (-̈e)** doctor

die **Ärztin (-nen)** doctor (*f.*)

die **Arzthelferin (-nen)** doctor's assistant

auch also, as well

auf on, onto, at; **auf Wiedersehen!** goodbye!; **auf Wiederhören!** goodbye! (on the phone)

der **Aufschnitt** sliced cold meats, sausage

aufstehen (*sep.*) to get up; **wann stehen Sie auf?** what time do you get up?

der **Augenblick (-e)** = **der Moment(-e)** moment

aus out, out of, from

der **Ausgang (-̈e)** exit, way out

ausgebucht fully booked

ausgeschildert marked with road signs

ausgezeichnet excellent

die **Auskunft (-̈e)** directory assistance

ausmachen (*sep.*) to arrange

ausrichten (*sep.*) to give someone a message

außerdem besides;

außerdem noch etwas? anything else?

ausverkauft sold out

das **Auto (-s)** car
die **Autobahn (-en)** expressway
    automatisch automatically

B

das **Bad (-̈er)** bath
    bald soon; **sobald wie möglich** as soon as possible
die **Bank (-en)** bank
der **Bahnhof (-̈e)** railroad station
die **Banane (-n)** banana
der **Barmann (-̈er)** bartender
    Bayern Bavaria
der **Beamte (n)** clerk, official (*m.*)
die **Beamtin (-nen)** clerk, official (*f.*)
    bedanken: ich bedanke mich thank you
    bedienen to serve; **sich bedienen** to help oneself
    bei (m) at (the)
das **Beispiel (-e)** example;
    zum Beispiel for example
    bekommen to get
das **Benzin** gasoline
der **Beruf (-e)** job, profession
die **Besprechung (-en)** meeting
    bestellen to order; **ich habe bestellt** I've ordered
    besten: wie komme ich am besten? what's the best way to?
    besuchen to visit
das **Bett (-en)** bed
    bezahlen to pay
das **Bier (-e)** beer
    bin: ich bin I am
    bis until, till; **bis zum/zur** up to (the); **von . . . bis . . .** from . . .
till . . .
    bissl (*s. Ger.*) see **bißchen**
    bißchen: ein bißchen a little/bit
    bitte please; **bitte sehr,**
    bitte schön you're welcome, (offering something) here you are; **bitte
    sehr?, bitte schön?** what can I do for you?, yes please
    bitten to ask

    blau blue
    bleiben to stay
    bleifrei lead-free (gasoline)
die **Bootsfahrt (-en)** boat trip
die **Bratkartoffel (-n)** fried potato
    brauchen to need; **ich bräuchte** I need, please
    braun brown
der **Brief (-e)** letter
die **Briefmarke (-n)** stamp
    bringen to bring, serve
das **Brötchen (-)** roll
das **Brot (-e)** bread
die **Brücke (-n)** bridge
das **Büro (-s)** office
die **Bushaltestelle (-n)** bus stop
die **Butter** butter

C

    ca (= circa) about
das **Café (-s)** café
der **Campingplatz (¨e)** campground
der **Champignon (-s)** mushroom
der **Cocktail (-s)** cocktail
die **Cola (-s)** coke

D

    da there; **den/die/das da** that one there; **da drüben** over there
    dabei with you
die **Dame (-n)** lady, madam
    Dank: herzlichen/schönen/vielen Dank! many thanks!; **danke, danke schön, danke sehr** thank you; **nein, danke** no thank you
    dann then
    darf: darf es die sein? is this one all right? (*lit.* may it be this one?) see **dürfen**
    das this, that, the
die **Dauer** duration
    dauern to last; **wie lange dauert die Fahrt?** how long does tₕ

journey take?

dazu   with it, in addition

dem, den, der   the, this/that one

denn   for, because, then

das **Dessert (-s)**   dessert

deutsch   German

das **Deutschlernen**   the learning of German

die   the, that

diese, diesem, diesen, dieser   this, these

die **Dillkartoffel (-n)**   dill potato

direkt   direct(ly)

die **DM (D-Mark), Deutsche
Mark**   German currency

doch   yes (in answer to a negative question)

das **Doppelzimmer (-)**   double room

dort   there

die **Dose (-n)**   can

drauf (short for **darauf**)   on it; **das kommt drauf an**   it depends (on)

dreimal   three times, three (of)

dritte   third

die **Drogerie (-n)**   chemist's

drüben, da drüben   over there

durch   through

durchstellen (*sep.*) = **verbinden**   to connect, put through

die **Durchwahl(nummer) (-n)**   direct telephone number

dürfen   to be allowed; **darf ich?**   may I?; **dürfte ich?**   might/could I?

die **Dusche (-n)**   shower

E

der **Edamer**   Edam cheese

die **Ecke (-n)**   corner

das **Ei (-er)**   egg

ein, eine, einen, einer, einem   a, one

einbiegen (*sep.*)   to turn into

einfach   simple, simply; **einfache Fahrt**   one-way trip

einkaufen (*sep.*)   to go shopping

einlösen   to cash

einmal   once, one (ticket)

einsteigen (*sep.*)   to board
eintragen (*sep.*): **sich eintragen**   to register, put your name down
das **Einzelzimmer (-)**   single room
das **Eis**   ice, ice cream
der **Elbtunnel (-)**   Elbe tunnel
der **Empfang (¨e)**   reception
die **Empfangsdame (-n)**   receptionist (*f*)
empfehlen   to recommend
das **Ende (-n)**   end
der **Engländer (-)**   English(man)
die **Engländerin (-nen)**   English(woman)
entlang   along
entschuldigen: entschuldigen Sie! Entschuldigung!   excuse me
erste, erster   first; **erstmal** first of all
der **Erwachsene (-n)**   adult
es   it
das **Essen (-)**   meal
essen   to eat
die **Etage (-n)**   story, floor
etwa   about
etwas   something; **noch etwas?**   anything else?
der **Exportleiter (-)**   export manager (*m.*)
die **Exportleiterin (-nen)**   export manager (*f.*)
extra   special, additional

F

fahren   to drive, go (by transportation), travel
das **Fahrrad (¨er)**   bicycle
die **Fahrt (-en)**   trip
fährt ab   leaves
das **Fahrzeug (-e)**   vehicle
die **Familie (-n)**   family
die **Farbe (-n)**   color
fein   fine
das **Fenster (-)**   window
die **Ferien** (*pl.*)   holidays, vacation
fertigmachen (*sep.*)   to prepare

das **Filet (-s)** filet
finden to find
die **Firma (Firmen)** company
der **Fisch (-e)** fish
die **Flasche (-n)** bottle
das **Fleisch** meat
der **Flughafen (¨)** airport
fönen to blow dry
die **Frage (-n)** question
das **Fräulein (-)** Miss
der **Frankenwein (-e)** Franconian wine
die **Frau (-en)** woman; **Frau Peters** Mrs Peters
frei free; **haben Sie ein Zimmer frei?** have you got a room available?
fremd strange; **ich bin hier fremd** I'm a stranger here
die **Freesie (-n)** freesia
der **Freund (-e)** friend
frisch fresh
der **Friseur (-e)** hairdresser, barber
früh early; **morgen früh** tomorrow morning
das **Frühstück (-e)** breakfast
frühstücken to have breakfast
das **Frühstücksbüffet (-s)** breakfast buffet
für for
der **Fuß (¨e)** foot; **zu Fuß** on foot
die **Fußgängerpassage (-n)** pedestrian underpass

G

ganz quite
der **Garten (¨)** garden
der **Gast (¨e)** guest
die **Gaststätte (-n)** bar, inn
das **Gebäude (-)** building
geben to give
gebraten fried
gefällt: gefällt es Ihnen? do you like it?
gegen . . . Uhr at about . . . o'clock

gehen to go, walk; **es geht** not too bad; **das geht** that's possible; **wann geht die nächste . . .?** when is the next . . .?

gekocht, gekochten cooked

gelb yellow

das **Gemüse** vegetables

genug enough

geöffnet open

gerade just

das **Gepäck** luggage

geradeaus straight ahead

gern, gerne gladly; yes please, fine

geschmeckt: hat es Ihnen geschmeckt? did you enjoy it?

geschnitten sliced

gestern yesterday

gesund healthy

die **Getränkekarte (-n)** drinks menu

gewählt chosen

gibt: gibt es? is there?

ginge: das ginge that would be possible

das **Glas (⁻er)** glass

glauben to think

gleich in a minute, just; **gleich hier vorne** just in front here

gleichfalls the same to you

das **Gleis (-e)** platform

GmbH = Gesellschaft mit beschränkter Haftung Ltd

der **Gott (⁻er)** god

das **Gramm (-e)** gram

der **Grill (-s)** grill

groß, großen, großer, großes large, big

Großbritannien Great Britain

grün green

grüß: grüß Gott! (*s. Ger.*) greeting

die **Gulaschsuppe (-n)** goulash soup

gut, gute, guten good, fine, well

gute Nacht! good night!;

guten Abend! good evening!; **guten Morgen!** good morning!;

guten Tag! good day!

H

der Haarschnitt (-e) hairdo, haircut
haben to have
hatte: ich hatte I had
hätte: ich hätte gern(e) . . . I'd like . . .; **was hätten Sie gern(e)?** what would you like?

die Hafenrundfahrt (-en) trip around the harbor
halb, halbes half; **halb fünf** half past four; **ein halbes Pfund** half a pound, 250 grams
hallo! hello!
halten, sich halten (*refl.*) to keep (to); **halten Sie sich rechts** keep to the right

der Hauptbahnhof (-̈e) main railway station
der Hauptgang (-̈e) = das Hauptgericht (-e) main course
das Haus (-̈er) house; **nach Hause** (to) home
das Heilbuttsteak (-s) halibut steak
heiß hot
heißen to be called; **ich heiße** my name is; **wie heißen Sie?** what's your name?
helfen to help
herein in
der Herr (-en) sir, gentleman;
Herr Meier Mr Meier
die Herrschaften (*pl.*) ladies and gentlemen
herzlich hearty; **herzlich willkommen!** you're very welcome!
heute today
hier here
die Himbeertorte (-n) raspberry flan
hinein in, into
hin und zurück round-trip (*lit.* there and back)
hinüber across
hinunter down
historisch historical
hoch up
das Hochhaus (-̈er) skyscraper
der Holländer (Käse) Dutch (cheese)
holländisch Dutch
das Hotel (-s) hotel

hübsch pretty

I

ich I
ihn him, it
Ihnen (to) you
Ihr, Ihre, Ihren, Ihrem, Ihrer your
im = in dem in (the)
immer always
in in
in Ordnung all right, OK
der **Ingenieur (-e)** engineer
die **Innenstadt (¨e)** center of town, downtown
die **Insel (-n)** island
ist is
Italien Italy

J

ja yes
das **Jägerschnitzel (-)** pork cutlet 'hunter style' (in chasseur sauce)
das **Jahr (-e)** year

K

der **Kaffee (-s)** coffee
kann can; **was kann ich für Sie tun?** what can I do for you?
das **Kännchen (-)** small pot
die **Kantine (-n)** (company) lunchroom
der **Käse (-)** cheese
das **Käseomelett (-e** or **-s)** cheese omelet
die **Kasse (-n)** cashier's desk/or counter
der **Kassierer (-)** cashier
die **Karte (-n)** card, postcard, ticket
kaufen to buy
der **Keks (-e)** cookie
der **Keller (-)** cellar
der **Kellner (-)** waiter

die **Kellnerin (-nen)** waitress
das **Kilo(gramm)** kilo(gram)
der **Kilometer** kilometer
das **Kind (-er)** child
die **Kirche (-n)** church
die **Klasse (-n)** class
   klein, kleinen, kleiner, kleines small
das **Kleingeld** small change
   klingen to sound; **das klingt gut** that sounds good
der **Knoblauch** garlic
   Köln Cologne
   kombiniert combined
das **Komma (-ta** *or* **-s)** comma
die **Konditorei (-en)** café, pastry shop
   kommen (aus) to come (from)
die **Konferenz (-en)** conference, meeting
   können to be able; **können Sie?** can you?
der **Kopfsalat (-e)** lettuce
   kosten to cost
die **Krabbe (-n)** prawn
die **Krabbensuppe (-n)** prawn soup
die **Krebssuppe (-n)** crayfish soup
die **Kreditkarte (-n)** credit card
der **Kuchen (-)** cake
der **Kuchenbon (-s)** cake ticket
der **Kunde (-n)** customer (*m.*)
die **Kundin (-nen)** customer (*f.*)
die **Kunsthalle (-n)** art gallery
das **Kunstmuseum (-museen)** art museum
der **Kurze (-n)** 'shot' (of whiskey or liquor)
die **Kutterscholle (-n)** type of large plaice

<hr>

L

das **Labskaus** Hamburg sailor's stew
das **Land (-̈er)** country
   lang long; **wie lange?** how long?
der **Leberwurst (-̈e)** liver sausage

der **Lehrer (-)** teacher (*m.*)
die **Lehrerin (-nen)** teacher (*f.*)
   lieber rather, preferably
   leid: (das) tut mir leid I'm sorry
   leider unfortunately
   liegen to be situated, lie
   links (on, to the) left; **auf der linken Seite** on the left-hand side
der *or* das **Liter (-)** liter

M

   machen to make, do; **wird gemacht!** right away!; **was macht das?** how much is it?
das **Mädchen (-)** girl
das **Mal (-e)** time(s); **das vierte Mal** the fourth time
   Mallorca Majorca
   man one; **wo kann man?** where can one?
   manchmal sometimes
der **Mann (¨er)** man
die **Mark (-)** mark (German currency)
die **Marmelade (-n)** jam
   mehr more
   mehrere several
   mein, meine, meiner my
   meistens mostly
der *or* das **Meter (-)** meter
das **Menü (-s)** set-price meal
   mich me
die **Milch** milk
die **Million (-en)** million
das **Mineralwasser (¨)** mineral water
die **Minibar (-s)** minibar
die **Minute (-n)** minute
   mir (to) me
   mit with; **mit dem Bus** by bus
   mitreisen (*sep.*) to join the trip
das **Mittagessen (-)** lunch
die **Mittagspause (-n)** lunch

die **Mitte (-n)** middle; **Mitte März** mid March

möchte: ich möchte I'd like

möchten: wir möchten we'd like; **möchten Sie . . .?** would you like . . . ?

mögen to like

möglich possible

die **Mokkatorte (-n)** coffee-flavored cake

der **Moment (-e)** moment;

einen Moment, bitte just a moment, please

der **Monat (-e)** month

der **Morgen (-)** morning;

guten Morgen! good morning! **morgen** tomorrow; **morgen früh** tomorrow morning

die **Mosel** (river) Moselle; **der Moselwein** Moselle wine

München Munich

muß: ich muß I must/have to

müssen to have to

N

nach: Viertel nach acht quarter past eight; **nach Bremen** to Bremen

der **Nachmittag (-e)** afternoon

nachmittags in the afternoons

nachsehen (*sep.*) to check

die **Nacht (̈-e)** night; **gute Nacht!** good night

der, die, das **nächste** nearest, next

die **Nähe: hier in der Nähe** near here, nearby, in the vicinity

der **Name (-n)** name

natürlich of course

nebenan nearby, right here (*lit.* next door)

nee (*col.*) see **nein**

nehmen to take; **ich nehme Tee** I'll have tea

nein no; **nein, danke** no, thank you

nett nice

neu new

nicht not

nichts nothing

noch also, still; **auch noch** as well; **noch etwas?** anything else?;
noch zwei Bier two more beers
nochmal again
die **Nordsee** North Sea
normalerweise usually
Norwegen Norway
die **Nummer (-n)** number
nur only
die **Nußtorte (-n)** nut cake

der **Ober (-)** waiter
oder or
die **Öffnungszeiten** (*pl.*) opening hours
oft often
ohne without
die **Oma (-s)** grandma
der **Orangensaft (-̈e)** orange juice
Ordnung: in Ordnung! OK!, fine (*lit.* in order)
organisieren to organize
der **Ort (-e)** place
der **Ost(en)** east

paar: ein paar a few
das **Paket (-e)** package, pack
das **Papiertaschentuch (-̈er)** paper tissue
der **Park (-s)** park
parken to park
das **Parkhaus (-̈er)** parking garage
der **Passagier (-e)** passenger
der **Passant (-en)** passer-by (*m.*)
der **Paß (-ässe)** passport
paßt: was paßt? what fits/suits?
der **Patient (-en)** patient (*m.*)
die **Patientin (-nen)** patient (*f.*)
die **Person (-en)** person

der **Personalchef (-s)**   personnel manager
der **Personenzug (⁻e)**   slow local train
die **Petersilie**   parsley
der **Pfennig (-e)**   pfennig (German currency)
der **Pfirsich (-e)**   peach
die **Pfirsichtorte (-n)**   peach flan
der **Pförtner (-)**   doorman, porter
das **Pfund (-e)**   pound, half a kilo
der **Pinguin (-e)**   penguin
der **PKW (Personenkraftwagen) (-)**   car
der **Plan (⁻e)**   map, plan;
   Großer Plan   name of street in Celle
der **Platz (⁻e)**   seat, place, space
der **Platzwart (-e)**   campground manager
der **Polizist (-en)**   policeman
die **Pommes frites** (pl.)   French fries
die **Post**   post office
das **Postamt (⁻er)**   post office
die **Postkarte (-n)**   postcard
   pro   per
der **Produktmanager (-)**   product manager
das **Produktmeeting (-s)**   product meeting
   prost!   cheers

R

die **Rechnung (-en)**   bill, check
   recht   correct, right
   rechts   (on, to the) right; **auf der rechten Seite**   on the right-hand side
die **Regel (-n)**   rule; **in der Regel**   as a rule
   reif   ripe
   rein: kommen Sie rein   come in
die **Reise (-n)**   journey, trip
der **Reisescheck (-s)**   traveler's check
   reservieren   to reserve
das **Restaurant (-s)**   restaurant
der **Rheinwein (-e)**   Rhine wine
die **Rose (-n)**   rose
   rot   red

der **Rotwein (-e)** red wine
der **Ruhetag (-e)** rest day
das **Rumpsteak (-s)** rump steak
    runter (short for **herunter**) down here

S

    sagen to say
die **Sahne** cream
das **Sahnesteak (-s)** steak with cream sauce
der **Salat (-e)** salad
das **Sanatorium (-ien)** sanatorium
die **Sardine (-n)** sardine
    schade! what a pity!
das **Schauspielhaus (-̈er)** theater, playhouse
das **Schild (-er)** sign
der **Schinken (-)** ham
    schlecht bad
das **Schloß (-̈sser)** castle
der **Schlüssel (-)** key
    schmecken to taste; **hat es Ihnen geschmeckt?** did you enjoy it?
der **Schnaps (-̈e)** schnaps
    schneiden to cut, slice; **geschnitten** sliced
    schnell quick(ly); **wie komme ich am schnellsten?** what's the quickest way?
die **Schnellbahn = S-Bahn (-en)** fast local train system
das **Schnitzel (-)** cutlet
die **Schokolade (-n)** (hot) chocolate
die **Scholle (-n)** plaice
    schon already
    schön nice, lovely, beautiful; **bitte schön?** yes, please?; **bitte schön!** you're welcome, not at all!
    schönen Dank! many thanks!
der **Schotte (-n)** Scot(sman)
die **Schottin (-nen)** Scot(swoman)
    schreiben to write
das **Schwarzbrot (-e)** (black) rye bread
die **Schwarzwälder Kirschtorte (-n)** 'Black Forest' cherry cake
    schwierig difficult

sehen to see

sehr very; **bitte sehr!** you're welcome, not at all!

sein to be

die **Seite (-n)** side; **auf der rechten/linken Seite** on the right/left-hand side

das **Sekretariat (-e)** secretary's office

die **Sekretärin (-nen)** secretary (f.)

selbst tanken to serve oneself with gasoline

das **Seminar (-e)** seminar

der **Senatorentopf** meat and vegetable dish

sich oneself, yourself

sicher(lich) sure(ly), certain(ly)

sie they, she, it

Sie you (formal)

sind: Sie/wir/sie sind you/we/they are

der **Skat** card game

so so; **so . . . wie . . .** as . . . as . . .

sofort right away

der **Sohn (¨e)** son

sollen to be supposed to; **sollte: sollte ich?** should I?

sonnabends on Saturdays

die **Sonne (-n)** sun

sonst: sonst noch etwas? anything else?

sonntags on Sundays

die **Sorte (-n)** sort, kind, type

Spanien Spain

der **Spaß (¨e)** joke, fun; **viel Spaß!** have fun

spät late

spazierengehen (sep.) to go for a walk

die **Speisekarte (-n)** menu

spielen to play

speisen to eat, dine

sprechen to speak

der **Stadtplan (¨e)** city map

die **Stadtrundfahrt (-en)** city sightseeing tour

der **Statistiker (-)** statistician (m.)

stehen to stand, to be

stellen to put

stimmt: das stimmt so that's all right
die **Straße (-n)** street
die **Straßenbahn (-en)** streetcar
das **Stück (-e)** piece (of), item
die **Stunde (-n)** hour
der **Süden** south
das **Super** super (grade of gasoline)
der **Supermarkt (ˉe)** supermarket

T

der **Tag (-e)** day; **guten Tag!** *lit.* good day!
die **Tagessuppe (-n)** soup of the day
täglich daily
die **Tagung (-en)** meeting, conference
der **Tankwart (-e)** service-station attendant
die **Tasche (-n)** pocket
die **Tasse (-n)** cup
die **Taxe (-n)** or **das Taxi (-s)** taxi
der **Taxifahrer (-)** taxi-driver (*m.*)
die **Taxifahrerin (-nen)** taxi-driver (*f.*)
der **Tee (-s)** tea
die **Teewurst (ˉe)** type of sausage
telefonieren to telephone
die **Telefonnummer (-n)** telephone number
die **Telefonzelle (-n)** telephone booth
das **Tennis** tennis
der **Termin (-e)** appointment
der **Terminkalender (-)** diary, appointment book
der **Tisch (-e)** table
die **Tochter (ˉ)** daughter
die **Toilette (-n)** toilet
die **Tomate (-n)** tomato
der **Topf (ˉe)** pot
der **Tourist (-en)** tourist (*m.*)
traditionell traditional
die **Traube (-n)** grape
treffen to meet; **sich treffen** (refl.)**: wo treffen wir uns?** where shall we meet?

die **Treppe (-n)** steps, staircase
trinken to drink
trocken dry
tschüs! (*col.*) bye-bye!
tun to do; **was kann ich für Sie tun?** what can I do for you?

U

die **U-Bahn Station (-en)** subway station
über across, over, via
überlegen to think
Uhr: wieviel Uhr ist es? what time is it?
um at; **um ... Uhr** at ... o'clock; **um die Ecke** around the
corner
umsteigen (*sep.*) to change (train, streetcar, bus)
und and
ungarisch Hungarian
ungefähr about
uns (to) us
unten down below
unterschreiben to sign
die **Unterschrift (-en)** signature
der **Urlaub (-e)** holiday, vacation
usw = und so weiter and so on, etc.

V

das **Vanille-Eis** vanilla ice cream
die **Veranstaltung (-en)** event
verbinden to connect
verfügung: zur verfügung available
verheiratet married
der **Verkäufer (-)** salesclerk, vendor (*m.*)
die **Verkäuferin (-nen)** salesclerk, vendor (*f.*)
verschieden different
der **Vertreter (-)** representative (*m.*)
die **Vertreterin (-nen)** representative (*f.*)
der **Verwalter (-)** manager
viel much, a lot
viele many; **vielen Dank!** many thanks

vielleicht perhaps

viermal four times, four (of)

vierte fourth

das **Viertel (-)** quarter

voll full up

volltanken (*sep.*) to fill up (with gasoline)

von of, from

vor to, in front of, before

vorab to start with

der **Vormittag (-e)** morning

vormittags in the morning(s)

vorn(e) in front

der **Vorname (-n)** first name

die **Vorspeise (-n)** appetizer, hors d'oeuvre

vorstellen to introduce

die **Vorwahl(nummer) (-n)** dialing code, prefix

W

wählen to choose

war, wäre, waren was, would be

wann? when?

was für . . . ? what kind of . . . ?

was? what? **was hätten Sie gerne?** what would you like?

waschen to wash

das **Wasser (-)** water

der **Wattwagen (-)** horse-drawn cart used to cross mud flats

wechselhaft changeable

wegen for, because of

wegfahren (*sep.*) to go away; **fahren Sie weg?** do you go away?

weichgekochtes: ein weichgekochtes Ei a soft-boiled egg

der **Wein (-e)** wine

die **Weinkarte (-n)** wine list

die **Weintraube (-n)** grape

weiß white

der **Weißwein (-e)** white wine

weit far

weiter (further) on

welcher?, welche?, welchem? which?

wenn if, when; **wenn es geht** if possible

die **Werbeabteilung(en)** publicity department

der **West (-en)** west

das **Wetter** weather

der **Widerwille** reluctance, disgust

wie? how? what? **wie geht's?** how are you?; **wie komme ich . . . ?** how do I get . . . ?

wie lange? how long?

wieder again

Wiederhören: auf Wiederhören! goodbye! (on the phone)

Wiedersehen: auf Wiedersehen! goodbye!

wieviel? how much?; **wie viele?** how many?

willkommen welcome

der **Winter** winter

wir we

der **Wirt (-e)** landlord, proprietor

wo? where?; **wo gibt es . . . ?** where is there . . . ?

woandershin (to go) somewhere different

die **Woche (-n)** week

das **Wochenende (-n)** weekend

woher? where from?

wohin? where (to)?

Wohl: zum Wohl! cheers!, your health!

wohnen to live

der **Wohnwagen (-)** motor home

wollen to wish, want; **wollen Sie mit?** do you want to join us?

wunderbar wonderful

der **Wunsch (-̈e)** wish

würden: ich würde gern (e) I'd like; **würden Sie?** would you?

die **Wurst (-̈e)** sausage

Z

der **Zahnarzt (-̈e)** dentist (*m.*)

zeigen to show; **das kann ich Ihnen zeigen** I can show you that

das **Zelt (-e)** tent

die **Zeitung (-en)** newspaper

der **Zeltplatz (-̈e)**   campsite

ziemlich   fairly, rather

das **Zimmer (-)**   room

der **Zimmerausweis (-e)**   room card

die **Zimmernummer (-n)**   room number

der **Zimmerschlüssel (-)**   room key

zirka   about

die **Zitrone (-n)**   lemon

die **Zitronenbutter**   lemon butter

das **Zitronensorbet (-s)**   lemon sorbet

zu   to; **zu Ende**   over; **zu Fuß**   on foot; **zu sechzig** at sixty

der **Zug (-̈e)**   train

zur Verfügung   available

zum (= zu dem), zur (= zu der)   to the

zurück   back; **hin und zurück**   there and back, round-trip (ticket)

zusammen   together

zweimal   twice, two (of)

das **Zweipersonenzelt (-e)**   two-person tent

zweite   second

zwo = zwei   two

zwomal see **zweimal**

ENGLISH-GERMAN

A

a, one   ein, eine, eins, einen, einer, einem

about   ca (= zirka), etwa, ungefähr, zirka

across   über; **across (there)**   hinüber

additional   extra

address   die Adresse (-n), die Anschrift (-en)

adult   der Erwachsene (-n)

afternoon   der Nachmittag (-e); **in the afternoons**   nachmittags

again   nochmal, wieder

airport   der Flughafen (⸚)

all   alles; **that's all**   das ist alles; **all right** in Ordnung (*lit.* **in order**)

along   entlang

already   schon

also   auch

always   immer

American (man)   der Amerikaner (-); **American (woman)**   die Amerikanerin (-nen)

and   und; **and so on**   usw = und so weiter

answer   die Antwort (-en)

anything   etwas; **anything else?**   außerdem noch etwas?, noch etwas?, sonst noch etwas?

appetite   der Appetit

appetizer   die Vorspeise (-n)

apple   der Apfel (⸚); **apple pastry**   der Apfelstrudel (-)

appointment   der Termin (e); **appointment book**   der Terminkalender (-)

arrange   ausmachen *(sep.)*

art   die Kunst (⸚e); **art gallery**   die Kunsthalle (-n); **art museum**   das Kunstmuseum (-museen)

as   als; **as . . . as . . .**   so . . . wie . . .

ask   bitten

assistance, directory   die Auskunft (⸚e)

at   an; bei; um; **at about . . . o'clock**   gegen . . . Uhr; **at . . . o'clock**   um . . . Uhr

attendant, service-station   der Tankwart (-e)

automatically   automatisch

available   zur Verfügung

avenue   die Allee (-n)

B

back   zurück

bad   schlecht

banana   die Banane (-n)

barber   der Friseur (-e)

bartender   der Barmann (¨er)

bath   das Bad (¨er)

Bavaria   Bayern

be   sein; **you/we/they are**   Sie/wir/sie sind

be able   *see* can

be allowed   dürfen; **may I?**   darf ich?; **might/could I?**   dürfte ich?

be called   heißen; **my name is**   ich heiße; **what's your name?**   wie heißen Sie?

be situated   liegen

be supposed to   sollen; **should I?**   sollte ich?

beautiful   schön

because of   wegen

bed   das Bett (-en)

beer   das Bier (-e); **two more beers**   noch zwei Bier

before   vor

beginning   der Anfang (¨e)

besides   außerdem

beverages, list of   die Getränkekarte (-n)

bicycle   das Fahrrad (¨er)

big   groß, großen, großer, großes

bill   die Rechnung **(-en)**

blow dry   fönen

blue   blau

board   einsteigen *(sep.)*

booth, telephone   die Telefonzelle (-n)

bread   das Brot (-e); **(dark) rye bread**   das Schwarzbrot (-e); **roll**   das Brötchen (-)

breakfast   das Frühstück (-e); **breakfast buffet**   das Frühstücksbüffet (-s); **have breakfast**   frühstücken
bridge   die Brücke (-n)
bring   bringen
brown   braun
building   das Gebäude (-)
bus   der Bus (-se); **bus stop**   die Bushaltestelle (-n); **by bus**   mit dem Bus
but (also used for emphasis)   aber
butter   die Butter; **lemon butter**   die Zitronenbutter
buy   kaufen
bye-bye! *(col.)*   tschüs!

C

cafe   das Café (-s), die Konditorei (-en)
cake   der Kuchen (-), die Torte (-n); **"Black Forest" cherry cake**   die Schwarzwälderkirschtorte (-n); **cake ticket**   der Kuchenbon (-s); **coffee-flavored cake**   die Mokkatorte (-n); **nut cake**   die Nußtorte (-n)
call   anrufen *(sep.)* ; **telephone call**   der Anruf (-e)
campground   der Campingplatz (-̈e), der Zeltplatz (-̈e); **campground manager**   der Platzwart (-e)
campsite   der Campingplatz (-̈e), der Zeltplatz (-̈e)
can   die Dose (-n)
can (be able)   können; **can you?**   können Sie?; **what can I do for you?**   was kann ich für Sie tun?
canteen   die Kantine (-n)
car   das Auto (-s), der Wagen (-), der PKW (Personenkraftwagen)
caravan   der Wohnwagen (-)
card   die Karte (-n); **credit card**   die Kreditkarte (-n)
cart, horse-drawn, used to cross mud flats   der Wattwagen (-)
cash   einlösen
cashier   der Kassierer (-); **cashier's desk**   die Kasse (-n)
castle   das Schloß (-̈sser)
cellar   der Keller (-)
certain(ly)   sicher(lich)
change (train, streetcar, bus)   umsteigen *(sep.)*

changeable   wechselhaft

check   nachsehen *(sep.)*

check, traveler's   der Reisescheck (-s)

cheers!   zum Wohl!, prost!

cheese   der Käse (-); **cheese omelet**   das Käseomelett (-e *or* -s); **Dutch cheese**   der Holländer Käse; **Edam cheese**   der Edamer

child   das Kind (-er)

chocolate, hot chocolate   die Schokolade (-n)

choose   wählen

chosen   gewählt

church   die Kirche (-n)

city   die Stadt (¨e); **city map**   der Stadtplan (¨e); **city sightseeing tour**   die Stadtrundfahrt (-en)

class   die Klasse (-n)

clerk   der Beamte (-n) *(m.)*, die Beamtin (-nen) *(f.)*

cocktail   der Cocktail (-s)

code, dialing   die Vorwahlnummer (-n)

coffee   der Kaffee (-s)

coke   die Cola (-s)

Cologne   Köln

color   die Farbe (-n)

combined   kombiniert

come   kommen; **come from**   kommen . . . aus; **come in**   kommen Sie rein

comma   das Komma (-s *or* -ta)

company   die Firma (Firmen); **joint stock company**   AG = Aktiengesellschaft

conference   die Konferenz (-en), die Tagung (-en)

connect   durchstellen *(sep.)*, verbinden

cooked   gekocht

cookie   der Keks (-e)

corner   die Ecke (-n); **around the corner**   um die Ecke

cost   kosten

country   das Land (¨er); **another country**   ein anderes Land

course, main   der Hauptgang (¨e), das Hauptgericht (-e)

crayfish   der Krebs (-e); **crayfish soup**   die Krebssuppe (-n)

cream   die Sahne

credit   der Kredit (-e); **credit card**   die Kreditkarte (-n)
cup   die Tasse (-n)
customer   der Kunde (-n) *(m.)*, die Kundin (-nen) *(f.)*
cut   schneiden
cutlet   das Schnitzel (-); **pork cutlet "hunter style"**   das Jager-
  schnitzel

D

daily   täglich
daughter   die Tochter (¨)
day   der Tag (-e); *lit.* **good day!**   guten Tag!; **day of rest**   der Ruhetag
  (-e)
dentist *(m.)*   der Zahnarzt (¨e)
departure   die Abfahrt (-en)
department, publicity   die Werbeabteilung (-en)
dessert   das Dessert (-s)
did you enjoy it?   hat es Ihnen geschmeckt?
different   verschieden
difficult   schwierig
dill   der Dill (-e); **dill potato**   die Dillkartoffel (-n)
dine   speisen
dinner   das Abendessen (-)
direct(ly)   direkt
disgust   der Widerwille
do   tun; machen; **what can I do for you?**   was kann ich für Sie tun?
do you like it?   gefällt es Ihnen?
doctor   der Arzt (¨e) *(m.)*, die Ärztin (-nen) *(f.)*; **doctor's assistant** *(f.)*
  die Arzthelferin (-nen)
down   hinunter; **down below**   unten; **down here**   runter (*short for*
  herunter)
downtown   die Innenstadt (-e)
drink   trinken
drive   fahren
drugstore   die Drogerie (-n)
dry   trocken
duration   die Dauer
Dutch   holländisch; **Dutch cheese**   der Holländer Käse (-)

E

early   früh
east   Ost, der Osten
eat   essen, speisen
egg   das Ei (-er); **a soft-boiled egg**   ein weichgekochtes Ei
Elbe tunnel   der Elbtunnel (-)
employee   der *or* die Angestellte (-n)
end   das Ende (-n)
engineer   der Ingenieur (-e)
English(man)   der Engländer (-); **English(woman)**   die Engländerin
   (-nen)
enough   genug
etc.   usw = und so weiter
evening   der Abend (-e); **good evening**   guten Abend! **in the
   evenings**   abends
event   die Veranstaltung (-en)
everything   alles
example   das Beispiel (-e); **for example**   zum Beispiel
excellent   ausgezeichnet
excuse me   entschuldigen Sie!, Entschuldigung!
exit   der Ausgang (-̈e)
expressway   die Autobahn (-en)

F

fairly   ziemlich
family   die Familie (-n)
far   weit
few, a   ein paar
filet   das Filet (-s)
fill up (with gas)   volltanken *(sep.)*
find   finden
fine   fein
Fine!   in Ordnung! *(lit.* **in order**)
first   erste, erster; **first of all**   erstmal; **first name**   der Vorname (-n)
fish   der Fisch (-e)
flan, raspberry   die Himbeertorte (-n)

floor   die Etage (-n)

foot   der Fuß (¨-e); **on foot**   zu Fuß

for   für

for *(because of)*   wegen

for *(because, since; then)*   denn

four   vier; **four times**   viermal

fourth   vierte

Franconian wine   der Frankenwein (-e)

free   frei

freesia   die Freesie (-n)

French fries   die Pommes frites (pl.)

fresh   frisch

fried   gebraten; **fried potato**   die Bratkartoffel (-n)

friend   der Freund (-e) *(m.)*, die Freundin (-nen) *(f.)*

from   von; aus

full   voll

fun   der Spaß (-e); **have fun**   viel Spaß!

further   weiter

<hr>

G

garage, parking   das Parkhaus (¨-er)

garden   der Garten (¨-)

garlic   der Knoblauch

gasoline   das Benzin; **serve oneself with gasoline**   selbst tanken

gentleman   der Herr (-en)

German   deutsch

get   bekommen

get up   aufstehen *(sep.)*; **what time do you get up?**   wann stehen Sie auf?

girl   das Mädchen (-)

give   geben

give a message   ausrichten *(sep.)*

gladly   gern, gerne

glass   das Glas (¨-er)

go   gehen; fahren; **go home**   nach Hause gehen; **go somewhere different**   woandershin gehen; **go away**   wegfahren *(sep.)*; **go for a walk**   spazierengehen *(sep.)*; **go shopping**   einkaufen *(sep.)*

god   der Gott (¨er)

good   gut, gute, guten; **good day!**   guten Tag!; **good evening!** guten Abend!; **good morning!**   guten Morgen!; **good night!**   gute Nacht!

goodbye!   auf Wiedersehen!; *(on the phone)*   auf Wiederhören!

goulash soup   die Gulaschsuppe (-n)

gram   das Gramm (-e); **250 grams**   ein halbes Pfund

grandma   die Oma (-s)

grandpa   der Opa

grape   die Traube (-n), die Weintraube (-n)

Great Britain   Grossbritannien

green   grün

grill   der Grill (-s)

guest   der Gast (¨e)

H

haircut   der Haarschnitt (-e)

hairdresser   der Friseur (-e)

half   halb, halbes; **half past four**   halb funf; **half a pound**   ein halbes Pfund

halibut steak   das Heilbuttsteak (-s)

ham   der Schinken (-)

have   haben; **have to**   müssen

health   die Gesundheit; **healthy**   gesund; **to your health**! zum Wohl!

hearty   herzlich

hello!   hallo!

help   helfen

here   hier

him   ihn

historical   historisch

holiday   der Urlaub (-e); **holidays**   die Ferien *(pl.)*

hors d'oeuvre   die Vorspeise (-n)

hot   heiß; **hot chocolate**   die Schokolade (-n)

hotel   das Hotel (-s)

hour   die Stunde (-n); **opening hours**   die Öffnungszeiten *(pl.);* **what time is it?**   Wieviel Uhr is es?

house   das Haus (¨er)

how wie; **how are you?** wie geht's?; **how do I get . . . ?** wie komme ich . . . ?; **how long?** wie lange?; **how many?** wie viele?; **how much?** wieviel?; **how much is it?** was macht das?
Hungarian ungarisch

I ich; **I am** ich bin; **I had** ich hatte; **I must/have to** ich muß; **I'd like** ich möchte, ich hatte gern(e); **I'm sorry** (das) tut mir leid; **me** mich; **to me** mir; **my** mein, meine, meiner
ice das Eis
ice cream das Eis; **vanilla ice cream** das Vanille-Eis
if wenn
in in; herein; hinein; **in the** im = in dem; **in a minute** gleich
Inc./Ltd. GmbH = Gesellschaft mit beschränkter Haftung
in front vorn(e); **just in front here** gleich hier vorne; **in the afternoons** nachmittags; **in the evenings** abends; **in the mornings** vormittags
inn die Gaststätte (-n)
introduce vorstellen *(sep.)*
is ist; **is there?** gibt es?; **is this one all right?** darf es die sein?
island die Insel (-n)
it es
Italy Italien

jam die Marmelade (-n)
job der Beruf (-e)
joke der Spaß (¨e)
journey die Reise (-n); **join the trip** mitreisen *(sep.)*
juice, orange der Orangensaft (¨e)
just gerade

keep (to) halten, sich halten *(refl.)*; **keep to the right** halten Sie sich rechts

key   der Schlüssel (-); **room key**   der Zimmerschlüssel (-)
kilo(gram)   das Kilo(gramm)

L

lady   die Dame (-n); **ladies and gentlemen**   die Herrschaften *(pl.)*
landlord   der Wirt (-e)
large   groß, großen, großer, großes
last   dauern;
late   spät
lead-free (gasoline)   bleifrei
leave   abfahren *(sep.)*; **leaves**   fährt ab
left, on the   links; **on the left-hand side**   auf der linken Seite
letter   der Brief (-e)
lettuce   der Kopfsalat (-e)
lie   liegen
light, traffic   die Ampel (-n)
like   mögen
liter   der *or* das Liter (-)
little/bit, a   ein bißchen
live   wohnen
long   lang; **how long?**   wie lange?
lot, a   viel
lovely   schön
Ltd./Inc.   GmbH = Gesellschaft mit beschränkter Haftung
luggage   das Gepäck
lunch   das Mittagessen (-), die Mittagspause (-n)

M

Majorca   Mallorca
make   machen
man   der Mann (-̈er)
manager   der Verwalter; **export manager**   der Exportleiter (-) *(m.)*,
   die Exportleiterin (-nen) *(f.)*; **personnel manager**   der Personalchef
   (-s); **product manager**   der Produktmanager (-)
many   viele; **many thanks!**   herzlichen/schönen/vielen Dank!
map   der Plan (-̈e); **city map**   der Stadtplan (-̈e)

mark (German currency)   die Mark (-)
marked with road signs   ausgeschildert
married   verheiratet
me   mich; **to me**   mir
meal   das Essen (-); **set-price meal**   das Menü (-s); **enjoy your meal!**
   guten Appetit!
meat   das Fleisch; **sliced cold meats**   der Aufschnitt
meet   (sich) treffen; **where shall we meet?**   wo treffen wir uns?
meeting   die Besprechung (-en), die Konferenz (-en), die Tagung (-en);
   product meeting   das Produktmeeting (-s)
menu   die Speisekarte (-n); **list of beverages**   die Getränkekarte (-n)
meter   der *or* das Meter (-)
middle   die Mitte (-n); **mid-March**   Mitte März
milk   die Milch
million   die Million (-en)
minibar   die Minibar (-s)
minute   die Minute (-n)
Miss   das Fräulein (-)
moment   der Augenblick (-e), der Moment (-e); **just a moment,**
   please   einen Moment, bitte
money   das geld; **German currency**   die DM (D-Mark), Deutsche
   Mark
month   der Monat (-e)
more   mehr
morning   der Vormittag(e) der Morgen (-); **good morning!**   guten
   Morgen!; **in the mornings**   morgens; **tomorrow morning**
   morgen früh
Moselle (river)   die Mosel; **Moselle wine**   der Moselwein
mostly   meistens
much   viel
Munich   München
mushroom   der Champignon (-s)
my   mein, meine, meiner

N

name   der Vorname (-n); **first name**   der Vorname (-n); **my name is**
   ich heiße; **what's your name?**   wie heißen Sie?

nearby   hier in der Nähe

nearest   der, die, das nächste

need   brauchen; **I need, please**   ich bräuchte

new   neu

newspaper   die Zeitung (-en)

next   der, die, das nächste

nice   nett, schön; **that's very nice (of you)!**   das ist aber nett

night   die Nacht (¨e); **good night!**   gute Nacht!

no   nein, nee *(col.)*; **no, thank you**   nein, danke

no *(indef. pron.)*   kein, keine, keinen, keinem, keiner

North Sea   die Nordsee

Norway   Norwegen

not   nicht; **not too bad**   es geht

nothing   nichts

number   die Nummer (-n); **direct telephone number**   die Durchwahlnummer (-n); **telephone number**   die Telefonnummer (-n)

O

of   von; **of course**   natürlich

offer   anbieten *(sep.)*

office   das Büro (-s); **secretary's office**   das Sekretariat (-e)

official   der Beamte (-n), die Beamtin (-nen)

often   oft

oh   ach

OK!   in Ordnung *(lit.* **in order**)

old   alt; **old part of town**   die Altstadt (¨e)

on   auf; **on it**   drauf (= darauf); **it depends (on)**   das kommt drauf
an; **on Saturdays**   sonnabends; **on Sundays**   sonntags; **on Thursday**   am Donnerstag; **on foot**   zu Fuß

once   einmal

one   man; **where can one . . . ?**   wo kann man . . . ?

oneself   sich

only   nur

open   geöffnet

or   oder

order   bestellen; **I've ordered**   ich habe bestellt

organize   organisieren

other   andere

out   aus
over   über; **over there**   drüben, da drüben
over   zu Ende

package   das Paket (-e)
park   parken
park   der Park (-s)
parking garage   das Parkhaus ("-er)
parsley   die Petersilie
passenger   der Passagier (-e)
passer-by *(m.)* der Passant (-en)
passport   der Paß ("-asse)
pastry shop   die Konditorei (-en)
patient   der Patient (-en) *(m.)*, die Patientin (-nen) *(f.)*
pay   bezahlen
peach   der Pfirsich (-e); **peach flan**   die Pfirsichtorte (-n)
penguin   der Pinguin (-e)
per   à, pro
perhaps   vielleicht
person   die Person (-en)
pharmacy   die Apotheke (-n)
pick up   abholen
piece   das Stück (-e)
place   der Ort (-e); der Platz (-e)
plaice (European flounder)   die Scholle (-n); **type of large plaice**
  die Kutterscholle (-n)
plan   der Plan ("-e)
platform   das Gleis (-e)
play   spielen
please   bitte
pocket   die Tasche (-n)
policeofficer   der Polizist (-en) *(m.)*, die Polizistin (-nen)
postcard   die Ansichtskarte (-n), die Karte (-n)
pot   der Topf ("-e); **small pot**   das Kännchen (-)
potato   die Kartoffel (-n); **dill potato**   die Dillkartoffel (-n); **French
  fries**   die Pommes frites *(pl.)*; **fried potato**   die Bratkartoffel (-n)
pound   das Pfund (-e)

prawn   die Krabbe (-n); **prawn soup**   die Krabbensuppe (-n)
preferably   lieber
prepare   fertigmachen *(sep.)*
pretty   hübsch
profession   der Beruf (-e)
proprietor   der Wirt (-e)
put   stellen

Q

quarter   das Viertel (-); **quarter past eight**   Viertel nach acht
question   die Frage (-n)
quick(ly)   schnell; **what's the quickest way?**   wie komme ich am schnellsten?
quite   ganz

R

railroad station   der Bahnhof (¨e); **main railroad station**   der Hauptbahnhof (¨e)
rather   ziemlich; lieber
reception   der Empfang (¨e)
receptionist   *(f.)* die Empfangsdame (-n)
recommend   empfehlen
red   rot; **red wine**   der Rotwein (-e)
reluctance   der Widerwille
register   (sich) eintragen *(sep.)*
representative, sales   der Vertreter (-) *(m.)*, die Vertreterin (-nen) *(f.)*
reserve   reservieren; **fully booked**   ausgebucht
restaurant   das Restaurant (-s), die Gaststätte (-n)
right   recht; **(on, to the) right**   rechts; **keep to the right**   halten Sie rechts   **on the right-hand side**   auf der rechten Seite
right away   sofort; **right away!**   wird gemacht!
ripe   reif
room   das Zimmer (-); **double room**   das Doppelzimmer (-); **single room**   das Einzelzimmer (-); **room card**   der Zimmerausweis (-e); **room key**   der Zimmerschlüssel (-); **room number**   die Zimmer-

nummer (-n); **do you have a room available?** haben Sie ein Zimmer frei?

rose die Rose (-n)

rule die Regel (-n); **as a rule** in der Regel

same selb, gleich; **the same to you** gleichfalls

salad der Salat (-e)

salesclerk der Verkäufer (-) *(m.)*, die Verkäuferin (-nen) *(f.)*

sanatorium das Sanatorium (-ien)

sardine die Sardine (-n)

sausage die Wurst (¨e); **liver sausage** die Leberwurst (¨e); **type of soft sausage** die Teewurst (¨e)

say sagen

schnaps der Schnaps (¨e)

Scot(sman) der Schotte (-n); **Scot(swoman)** die Schottin (-nen)

seat der Platz (¨e)

second zweite

secretary *(f.)* die Sekretärin (-nen)

see sehen

seminar das Seminar (-e)

serve bedienen; **serve oneself** sich bedienen; **serve oneself with gasoline** selbst tanken

several mehrere

she sie

"shot" (of liquor) der Kurze (-n)

shopping, go einkaufen *(sep.)*

show zeigen; **I can show you that** das kann ich Ihnen zeigen

shower die Dusche (-n)

side die Seite (-n); **on the right-/left-hand side** auf der rechten/linken Seite

sign unterschreiben

sign das Schild (-er)

signature die Unterschrift (-en)

simple einfach; **simply** einfach

skat (type of card game) der Skat

skyscraper das Hochhaus (¨er)

slice   schneiden; **sliced**   geschnitten; **sliced cold meats**   der Aufschnitt

small   klein; **small change**   das Kleingeld

so   so; also

sold out   ausverkauft

something   etwas

sometimes   manchmal

son   der Sohn (-̈e)

soon   bald; **as soon as possible**   sobald wie moglich

sort   die Sorte (-n)

sorbet, lemon   das Zitronensorbet (-s)

sorry, I'm sorry   (das) tut mir leid

sound   klingen; **that sounds good**   das klingt gut

soup   die Suppe (-n); **crayfish soup**   die Krebssuppe (-n); **goulash soup**   die Gulaschsuppe (-n); **prawn soup**   die Krabbensuppe (-n); **soup of the day**   die Tagessuppe (-n)

south   der Süden

Spain   Spanien

speak   sprechen

special   extra

staircase   die Treppe (-n)

stamp   die Briefmarke (-n)

stand   stehen

station, subway   die U-Bahn-Station

statistician   der Statistiker (-)

stay   bleiben

steak   das Steak (-s); **halibut steak**   das Heilbuttsteak (-s); **rump steak**   das Rumpsteak (-s); **steak with cream sauce**   das Sahnesteak (-s)

steps   die Treppe (-n)

still   noch

story (of a building)   die Etage (-n)

straight ahead   geradeaus

strange   fremd; **I'm a stranger here**   ich bin hier frend

street   die Straße (-n)

streetcar   die Straßenbahn (-en)

sun   die Sonne (-n)

super (*grade of gasoline*)   das Super

supermarket   der Supermarkt (-̈e)

sure(ly)   sicher(lich)

T

table   der Tisch (-e)

take   nehmen; **I'll take (have) tea**   ich nehme Tee

taste   schmecken

taxi   die Taxe (-n) *or* das Taxi (-s)

taxi–driver   der Taxifahrer (-) *(m.)*, die Taxifahrerin (-nen) *(f.)*

tea   der Tee (-s)

teacher   der Lehrer (-) *(m.)*, die Lehrerin (-nen) *(f.)*

telephone   das Telefon (-e); **telephone booth**   die Telefonzelle (-n);
   telephone call   der Anruf (-e); **telephone number**   die Telefonnummer (-n); **direct telephone number**   die Durchwahlnummer
   (-n); **(make a) telephone (call)**   telefonieren

tennis   das Tennis

tent   das Zelt (-e); **two-person tent**   das Zweipersonenzelt (-e)

thank   danken; **many thanks!**   herzlichen/schönen/vielen Dank!;
   thank you   danke, danke schön, danke sehr, ich bedanke mich; **no
   thank you**   nein, danke

that   der, die, das; **that would be possible**   das ginge; **that's all right**
   das stimmt so; **that one there**   den/die/das da; **that's possible**   das
   geht

the   der, die, das, der, dem

theater   das Schauspielhaus (¨er)

then   dann

there   dort, da; **over there**   da drüben; **that one there**   den/die/das
   da

they   sie

think   glauben; überlegen

third   dritte

this   der, die, das; diese, diesem, diesen, dieser; **these**   diese, dieser

three   drei; **three times**   dreimal

through   durch

ticket   die Karte (-n)

time(s)   das Mal (-e); **the fourth time**   das vierte Mal; **three times**
   dreimal

tissue, paper   das Papiertaschentuch (¨er)

to   zu

today   heute

together   zusammen
toilet   die Toilette (-n)
tomato   die Tomate (-n)
tomorrow   morgen; **tomorrow morning**   morgen früh
too   auch
to start with   vorab
tourist *(m.)*   der Tourist (-en)
town   die Stadt (-̈e); **old part of town**   die Altstadt (-̈e)
traditional   traditionell
train   der Zug (-̈e); **fast local train system**   die Schnellbahn =
    S-Bahn (-en); **slow local train**   der Personenzug (-̈e)
traveler's check   der Reisescheck (-s)
trip   die Fahrt (-en), die Reise (-n); **boat trip**   die Bootsfahrt (-en);
    join the trip   mitreisen *(sep.)*; **one-way trip**   einfache Fahrt;
    round trip   hin und zurück; **trip around the harbor**   die Hafen-
    rundfahrt (-en)
tunnel, Elbe   der Elbtunnel (-)
turn (into)   einbiegen *(sep.)*
twice   zweimal
two   zwei, zwo

U

underpass, pedestrian   die Fußgängerpassage (-n)
unfortunately   leider
until   bis; **from . . . until . . .**   von . . . bis . . .
up   hoch
us   uns; **to us**   uns
usually   normalerweise

V

vacation   der Urlaub (-e), die Ferien *(pl.)*
vegetables   das Gemüse
vehicle   das Fahrzeug (-e)
very   sehr
via   über
visit   besuchen

W

waiter   der Kellner (-), der Ober (-)

waitress   die Kellnerin (-nen)

walk   gehen, spazieren; **go for a walk**   spazierengehen *(sep)*

want   wollen; **do you want to join us?**   wollen Sie mit?

was   war, waren

wash   waschen

water   das Wasser (-); **mineral water**   das Mineralwasser (-)

way out   der Ausgang (¨e)

we   wir; **we'd like**   wir möchten

weather   das Wetter

week   die Woche (-n)

weekend   das Wochenende (-n)

welcome   willkommen; **welcome!**   herzlich willkommen! **you're welcome!**   bitte schön!

west   der West(en)

what   was; **what would you like?**   was hätten Sie gerne?; **what fits/suits?**   was paßt?; **what kind of . . .**   was für . . .; **what time is it?**   wieviel Uhr ist es?; **what's the best way to?**   wie komme ich am besten?; **what a pity!**   schade!; **what can I do for you?**   bitte sehr?, bitte schön?

when   wenn; wann; **when is the next . . .?**   wann geht die nächste . . .?

where   wo; **where (to)?**   wohin; **where from?**   woher?; **where is there . . . ?**   wo gibt es . . . ?

which?   welcher?, welche?, welchem?

white   weiß; **white wine**   der Weißwein (-e)

window   das Fenster (-)

wine   der Wein (-e); **Franconian wine**   der Frankenwein (-e); **Moselle wine**   der Moselwein (-e); **red wine**   der Rotwein (-e); **white wine**   der Weißwein (-e); **wine list**   die Weinkarte (-n)

winter   der Winter

wish   der Wunsch (¨e)

wish   wollen

with   mit; **with you**   dabei; **with it**   dazu

without   ohne

woman   die Frau **(-en)**

wonderful   wunderbar
work   die Arbeit (-en); **work (at)**   arbeiten (bei)
would be   wäre
would you like?   möchten Sie?
write   schreiben

Y

year   das Jahr (-e)
yellow   gelb
yes   ja; *(in answer to a negative question)* doch
yesterday   gestern
you (formal)   Sie; **to you**   Ihnen; **would you?**   würden Sie?; **what would you like?**   was hätten Sie gern(e)?
your   Ihr, Ihre, Ihren, Ihrem, Ihrer
your health!   zum Wohl!
you're welcome!   bitte schön!
yourself   sich

NOTES

NOTES

N O T E S